ADVANCE PRAISE

"A truly unique book for parents. Yarona Boster emphasizes emotional security and role modeling as foundations for growth—progressive, enlightening, and essential."

—DR. KIM BURGESS, CLINICAL PSYCHOLOGIST
AND PARENTING EXPERT

"I absolutely loved this book! Its stories, clarity, and compassion make complex psychological ideas feel deeply human and easy to apply, reminding us that both parenting and emotional growth are lifelong, evolving journeys."

—DR. KARLA GARJAKA, EQ EXPERT AND GUT-BRAIN SPECIALIST

"What sets this book apart from so many others is a carefully crafted balance between professional insight and personal testimony. Expertly blending these allows the reader a much needed, grace-filled space for both empathetic connection and reflective growth."

—ROBERT HULSE, YOUTH PASTOR, EDUCATOR, AND LIFE COACH

"Unspoken Signals is a must-have for every parent. Yarona's vulnerability and expertise shine, guiding families to raise emotionally secure children together."

—MICHELLE HAYES, CERTIFIED MARRIAGE
COACH AND PODCAST HOST

UNSPOKEN SIGNALS

UNSPOKEN SIGNALS

Essential Parenting Skills to Raise Emotionally Secure Children

Yarona Boster

yb

YARONA BOSTER

UNSPOKEN SIGNALS

Essential Parenting Skills to Raise Emotionally Secure Children

FIRST EDITION

ISBN   978-1-5445-5190-6   *Hardcover*
      978-1-5445-5189-0   *Paperback*
      978-1-5445-5191-3   *Ebook*
      978-1-5445-5227-9   *Audiobook*

To my son, Connor: I am honored and humbled to be a guiding light for you in this world. You are the embodiment of joy, hope and love. You are my special Bean, and I will always be your Donkey. My soul is in awe of you, and my heart flows with endless love for you.

To my husband, Carl, for being my favorite support and anchor in this world. I never knew I needed you until I met you. The bonds of time, tests, triumphs, failures and losses wrap my heart forever with yours. I may not be able to promise to stop overstuffing the garbage can, but I can promise there is a space in my heart and body that will forever remain yours.

To my sister, Mori, my giggling partner in crime "stealing diamonds" on a cold winter's night; my BT, my LBS, my D/FD, and my favorite memory keeper. Even though we scare people with our "mind sharing" moments, I'll keep laughing when our sanity is questioned, because I'm so darn lucky to have you as a sister. Nertz to you!!

To my friends and the rest of my crazy, loving family, my niblings, cousins and those gone from this world who remain inked on my heart, the lessons I have learned from each of you will stand the test of time.

And to my parents, my Abba and Eema: You live on in every memory, every breath, every apple picked in season, every cherry blossom petal I cherish, every line in my face and hands. As long as I have breath left in me, you will too.

CONTENTS

Parenting Clarity & Support Conversations

A Complimentary 30-Minute Conversation

Parenting comes with questions we rarely say out loud,

the worries that keep us up at night,

the patterns we cannot quite name, the
moments we wish felt easier.

If this book has stirred something in you, I
would love to offer a space to explore it.

This is not a sales call.

It is a grounded, judgment free space to
talk about what matters most.

Your Invitation:

You are invited to a free 30 Minute Parenting
Clarity and Support Conversation.

This is a focused and compassionate space
designed to help you understand:

- where you are right now as a parent
- what you need most in this moment
- what may be getting in the way

Together, we will gently explore:

- the **signals** your child may be sending
through their behavior
- the **patterns** shaping your responses as a parent
- the places you feel **stuck, overwhelmed, or unsure**
- the kind of support that would help you
feel more confident and connected

You do not have to navigate this alone.

You deserve support.

Your child deserves a *grounded, empowered* parent.

Limited number of conversations available each month.

FOREWORD

**—by Dr. Chérie Carter-Scott
"The Mother of Coaching" and #1 New
York Times bestselling author of If Life
Is a Game, These Are the Rules and
Life IS a Game: Life Lessons Learned
Living the Rules for Being Human**

Success in parenting, much like success in life, is not accidental. It is the result of awareness, intention, and practice. Over the past five decades, I have witnessed countless individuals discover that the unspoken signals they send through words, tone, presence, and even silence, shape not only their relationships, but their legacy. That is why this book, *Unspoken Signals*, is so vital for every parent. It illuminates the invisible currents of parenting: those subtle cues that ripple across generations, often without our awareness of the messages being sent.

When I first encountered Yarona Boster and her work, I was struck by her authenticity. She writes not from theory alone, but from lived experience—truly walking the talk. As the daughter of a Holocaust survivor and a mother who endured profound abuse, Yarona grew up in a household where love and wounds intermingled. She knows firsthand the paradox of inheritance; how we carry both the gifts and the gaps of those who raised us. Rather than turning away from that complexity, she leaned into it. She studied early childhood development, psychology, and coaching, transforming her own story into a roadmap for others.

This book is not a manual in the traditional sense, because parenting, unfortunately, lacks a step-by-step guide. Instead, it is a conversation. Each chapter blends personal narrative, developmental insight, and practical reflection. From the authoritarian echoes of "Because I said so!" to the pendulum swinging between overprotection and permissiveness, Yarona traces the evolution of parenting styles with clarity and compassion. She shows us how connection, autonomy, and competency, the three core needs identified in the Self-Determination Theory, become the foundation for raising resilient, emotionally secure children.

What makes *Unspoken Signals* unique is its balance of vulnerability and wisdom. Yarona does not shy away from the hardest truths: the grief of becoming an orphan, the ache of watching her son discover independence, the tension between control and release. Yet she also offers hope. She reminds us that resilience is built in small, everyday moments—mealtimes, playtimes, bedtime stories, even car rides. She teaches us that connection is not about perfection, but about presence. That autonomy is not rebellion, but rehearsal. That competency is not about being the best, but about believing, "I can."

I remember her story about her son Connor, who once told her, "You'll always be here, in my heart." That simple statement captures the essence of this book: parenting is not about clinging, but about creating secure attachment that endures even in absence. It is about preparing our children not only for life with us, but for life beyond us. And it is about preparing ourselves, as parents, to let go with grace.

Yarona's expertise as a coach, speaker, and strategist shines through every page. She has spent nearly two decades guiding families, leaders, and communities to create environments of fairness, transparency, and emotional intelligence. Her voice is nurturing yet firm, poetic yet practical. She invites us to pause, reflect, and choose the signals we want to pass forward—with the humility of someone who admits she is still learning every day.

For parents, this book is a gift. It will help you notice the signals you send, both spoken and unspoken, and give you tools to shape them with intention. For coaches and leaders, it offers a model of how emotional intelligence and authentic connection can transform not only families, but organizations and communities. And for anyone who has ever wondered how to break cycles of trauma while preserving the seeds of love, it provides guidance, grace and hope.

I encourage you to read these pages with openness and curiosity. Let the stories move you. Allow the exercises to challenge you. Invite the reflections to remind you that parenting is not about perfection—it is about persistence, practice and progress. And most of all, trust that the legacy you leave is not measured in accolades or possessions, but in the emotional security you cultivate in your children.

Yarona Boster has written a book that is both timely and timeless. It speaks to the urgent need for parents to be more intentional in a world of distraction and noise, and it speaks to the eternal truth that love, presence, and resilience are the anchors of human development. As you turn the page, know that you are stepping into a journey of awareness, compassion, and transformation. The signals you send matter. With this book, you will learn how to make them count forever.

PREFACE

WHY "UNSPOKEN SIGNALS"?

Before we step into the heart of this book, I want to talk about the unspoken communication signals of parenting. By signals, I mean the verbal and non-verbal cues we send to our children—often without conscious awareness. These are the words we repeat because we once heard them from our own parents, the gestures and tones we fall into without thinking, and the everyday habits that silently shape how our children see themselves and the world.

Signals are powerful because they are not always intentional. A sigh of frustration, a sharp tone, or even a tense posture can communicate far more than we realize. Children absorb these cues quickly, often mirroring them back before they have the language to reflect on their meaning. In this way, signals become a kind of hidden curriculum: lessons passed down not through deliberate teaching, but through the unspoken exchanges of daily life.

EVERYDAY SIGNALS WE PASS ON

I'll admit, I can be a very reactive driver. While I do not chase other cars or cause accidents, I do get mouthy in my own vehicle. I mutter things like, "Could this driver go any slower?" or "Seriously, the speed limit is forty, not twenty-five!" The tension I carry in my shoulders is proof of how much stress I let in when I am behind the wheel.

One morning, while running late for school, I heard from the back seat: "Seriously, dude?! Move faster! What's wrong with you?!"

That was my wake-up call. My son had caught my signal. This moment was a clear example of social learning in action. Children absorb adult tone and embodied cues, sometimes reproducing them before they can reflect on their meaning.

I knew we needed what I call a "debrief." Not a lecture in the heat of the moment, but a calm conversation later, when emotions had settled. Because when feelings are at their peak, that is rarely the right time to teach or reflect.

My behavior signaled to my son that it was acceptable to express annoyance at other drivers. And if such patterns persist without reflection, they can normalize escalation over time.

THE DEEPER IMPACT OF WORDS

Signals are not only about what we do. They are also about what we say.

My mother hated how her parents spoke to her. They told her she was a bad daughter, a bad person, even mocked things she could not control, like her mouth size or overbite. She was determined not to repeat that with us. And yet, when she was stressed and overwhelmed, she sometimes did. At times she called me "garbage" and a "snotty, ungrateful child."

There is a world of difference between saying, "I am upset that you threw the ball and broke the lamp" and "You are a terrible child for breaking the lamp."

Looking back, I know my mother loved us. She did not intend to harm us. She simply did not have the tools or the language to behave differently. And she carried her own patterns and struggles, which ultimately shaped her parenting.

CHOOSING THE SIGNALS WE WANT TO SEND

This is why I wrote this book. My goal is to help you uncover the signals you are sending—to yourself, to your partner, and most importantly, to your children. With that awareness, you can begin to choose which signals you want to pass forward and which ones you want to gently set down.

I write this not only as a parent, but as someone who has spent nearly two decades immersed in the fields of early childhood, human development, psychology, and coaching. As an international speaker and consultant, I have guided families, leaders, and public speakers in understanding how communication signals shape connection, resilience, and growth. This book is grounded in both expertise and lived experience, designed to give you practical tools backed by developmental insight.

Unspoken signals are powerful. They shape how our children see themselves, how they adapt to the world, and how they carry resilience or wounds into adulthood. My hope is that this book will help you notice those signals with compassion and give you the practical tools to choose the ones you want to pass forward.

At the end of each chapter, you'll find questions to consider. They're intended to help you notice the signals you give off, including the ones you might not realize you're sending.

So, take a deep breath, step into the Introduction with me, and remember: We prepare the child for the road, not the road for the child.

A NOTE ON THE STORIES SHARED

Throughout this book, I share moments from my work with families and individuals. To honor their privacy, all client names and identifying details have been changed. The only real names you will encounter belong to my own family. The stories themselves remain true to the heart of the experiences that shaped them.

INTRODUCTION

There's No User Manual for This Model

Imagine a world where every parent knew exactly what they were doing.

Raising a human being to become competent, capable, and secure is no easy job. Parenting is one of the most difficult and most important roles many people will ever hold in their lives. And whether it feels fair or not, parents often find themselves judged by how they raise their children.

Yet no society requires people to read books or take classes on basic child development. No country requires its citizens to learn how to be a stable, healthy parent before they actually become one.

I know this firsthand. My father was a Holocaust survivor and my mother had been abused as a child. They each carried their own wounds into parenting, and my formative years reflected a mix of pain and love. There were moments of reactivity, arguments, and generational patterns that caused harm. But there were also generous hearts, deep affection, and family bonds that left indelible marks on my life.

My parents wanted to raise us differently than they had been raised, but they did not have the knowledge to create the emotionally stable home they longed for. Desire alone does not give us the knowledge to raise children. If it did, I would not be writing this book.

Over the last nearly twenty years, I have studied and worked in early childhood, human development, psychology, and coaching. As an international speaker and consultant, I have guided families, leaders, and public speakers in helping them recognize the signals they send—both spoken and unspoken—and in using those signals to build resilience, emotional intelligence, and authentic connection. This book is a blend of professional expertise and lived experience, designed to help you understand both the science and the art of parenting.

When we are not given the tools, do not know where to look for them, or do not have the time to practice with them, we often fall back on what we know from our own early years. That is why so many people either repeat the patterns they grew up with or swing to the opposite extreme.

Over the last forty to fifty years, the role of parenting itself has shifted dramatically, shaping not only families but entire societies. And that evolution matters, because knowledge is more than power; it's what gives us the awareness to make lasting progress and the capacity to create meaningful change in human development.

This book will offer knowledge in:

- Why we do what we do as parents.
- How and why our children respond the way they do.
- Which parenting methods produce the greatest success in raising stable, emotionally secure children.
- Why and how that will affect the people they become.

Along the way, I will also share a brief history on how we arrived at this juncture, where there seem to be more parenting styles than pens in my junk drawer. (It's an overwhelming junk drawer, seriously.)

My sister and I once joked that it would be amazing if every child came with a "user-specific manual." Imagine having step-by-step guidance for your child's unique needs from birth through adulthood! But children are not blank slates.

Scientists estimate that approximately half (forty to sixty percent) of a person's temperament and personality traits come from biology, while the other half is shaped by experience—the home, relationships, and daily environments.

Think of it like a car that has been designed to go 220 miles per hour, but is rarely driven that fast. Most of the time, it cruises at ordinary speeds. But one day, with conditions just right, the driver suddenly pushes it to 220. In the same way, our genetic predispositions are like that car's design. They set the potential. Yet it takes both the driver and the conditions—environment, relationships, stresses, and also support—to determine which aspects of that potential remain quiet and which ones become activated in real life.

When I learned this, it strengthened my commitment to giving parents practical knowledge. We cannot change genetics, but we can shape the environments and relationships that support development.

Wouldn't it be powerful to become more proactive instead of reactive as a parent? That is my aim with this book: to give you practical, realistic strategies you can use in everyday life and in higher stress moments, while recognizing that some situations may also require professional support.

Because while parenting is not the only responsibility you carry, it may be one of the most significant roles you will ever take on. You could be a king, president, doctor, or world leader, but the ripple effect you have as a parent will reach generations to come.

As you move through these chapters, you will notice a rhythm. Each chapter flows with stories and insights, then offers **Signals for Reflection** so you can pause and consider your own patterns, and finally wraps up with **Closing Thoughts** that gather the lessons into something you can carry forward. This structure is intentional.

Parenting is not about quick fixes, but about awareness, reflection, and practice. The exercises and suggestions in this book are designed for everyday practice and do not replace clinical evaluation or treatment when concerns require it. My hope is that this book feels less like a textbook and more like a conversation, one that equips you with both knowledge and compassion as you walk the path of raising connected, capable and deeply secure children.

CHAPTER 1

THE PARENTING STYLES WE INHERITED

The Paradox of Inheritance

BECAUSE I SAID SO

I still remember the first time I heard the words, "Because I said so." I was young, standing in the kitchen, asking a question I thought was reasonable. The answer came back sharp and final, leaving no room for curiosity, no space for dialogue. In that moment, I felt the weight of authority without explanation. It was one of the earliest signals I received about how power worked in my home and what was expected of me as a child.

It wasn't just my parents. Friends' parents said it too. Teachers. Neighbors. It was the air we breathed as children: Adults knew best, children obeyed. That was the model many of us inherited. Keep in mind, parenting varies across cultures and households. What I describe was common in my experience, but didn't fit every household of the time.

And yet, even as a child, I sensed something was missing. I

longed for boundaries that felt safe, not suffocating. I wanted rules that made sense, not rules that shifted without warning. I wanted to understand, not just comply. Those longings were signals too, quiet indicators of what my developing self needed, but did not yet have the words to express.

That longing is what eventually led me to study parenting styles, to look back at my own family, and to ask the deeper questions: How did we get here? Why do so many of us repeat patterns we swore we would never pass on? And most importantly, how can we do better for the next generation?

THE PARENTING STYLES WE INHERITED

"Because I said so and I'm your parent."

"Spare the rod, spoil the child."

"It's 10:00 p.m., do you know where your children are?"

These phrases were more than cultural catchalls. They were signals of an era, shorthand for a parenting style rooted in authority, fear, and unquestioned obedience. They carried the weight of generations who believed that control equaled safety, that discipline equaled love, and that unquestioned respect for authority was the only way to prepare children for the world.

With nearly two decades in early childhood development and life coaching, as well as deep study of the psychology of human development, I have seen what can happen when the stress of being human and the role of parenting collide in destructive ways. The result is often a child's trauma carried silently into adulthood, shaping not only individuals but entire family systems for generations to come.

I also knew my parents wanted to raise their kids differently than they had been raised. They wanted to break the cycles and soften the harsh edges of their own childhoods. Desire alone, however, is not a parenting roadmap. And as an adult, I wanted to understand why their intentions didn't always translate into skill, and what it would take for me to parent differently.

When I first started to explore what made my parents tick, it began with a book. I found *Conversations with My Father* and used it to interview my father, to uncover who he was, what shaped him, and why. As a natural storyteller, he loved the process. The questions opened doors to stories I had never heard, stories that revealed the tension between who he longed to be as a parent and the limitations of what he had learned.

What I discovered was both simple and profound: My parents did not want to raise us in the fear-based, authoritarian style that had dominated their own families for generations. They wanted something different. But wanting and knowing how are not the same thing. Desire without tools often leads to inconsistency, and inconsistency can be just as destabilizing for a child as rigidity. Children read those inconsistencies as signals, often interpreting them as unpredictability or instability long before they can articulate what feels off.

This is the paradox so many parents face. We inherit not only the wounds of our upbringing but also the models of parenting we witnessed and experienced. Even when we vow to do things differently, we often find ourselves pulled back toward the familiar, repeating patterns we swore we would never pass on. It's also important to note that parenting outcomes are shaped by many factors—trauma, environment, resources, community support—and not any single cause, which means change is possible with awareness and the right support.

MY FATHER: THE FUN PARENT

My father's passivity and desire to be the "fun parent" made it hard to find fault in him when I was a child. All children want a fun parent, and he was the kinder, gentler one, except when he got into yelling matches with my mother. He often defaulted to "ask your mother" so he did not have to enforce the rules.

Even though he wanted us to have a strict schedule for things like dinnertime, which was how his adoptive parents raised him in their German household, he could not voice why it mattered or plan how to implement it. Rules lived in his memory as something important, but he lacked the language and confidence to translate them into daily life with his own children.

What makes his story more complex is that he was not always passive. After his adoption, especially in his teen years, he became something of a mischief-maker. He pushed boundaries, tested authority, and found small ways to reclaim a sense of control after years of surviving trauma. Mischief was his rebellion, but also his creativity. It was how he carved out space for himself in a world that had once stripped him of safety and choice.

Raised by emotionally cut-off adoptive parents after his traumatic five-year escape from Poland during the Holocaust, he carried wounds that shaped every part of his parenting. He had survived by staying quiet when necessary, but also by finding moments to bend the rules. In adulthood, that survival strategy translated into a longing to be loved at all costs. He wanted to be the parent we ran toward, not the one we feared.

But here is the dilemma: When a parent avoids setting boundaries in order to be loved, the child may feel affection but not always safety. I adored my father's gentleness and his playful spirit, but I also felt the absence of his authority. His refusal to step fully into the role of boundary-setter left my mother to carry the weight of discipline alone, which created its own imbalance. Children pick up on that imbalance quickly, often sensing the unspoken signals about who holds power, who avoids conflict, and where the emotional load falls in a family.

Looking back, I can see that his mischief was both a strength and a limitation. It gave him humor, lightness, and a sense of fun that I cherished. But it also meant that he sometimes treated rules as optional, which left me yearning for the structure he could not provide.

MY MOTHER: THE RELUCTANT DISCIPLINARIAN

My mother grew up as an only child under harsh dictates that left little room for individuality or self-worth: "Your profession will be one of these acceptable choices." "You are a terrible waste of space." "You got an A–? Why not an A+?"

She was not just criticized, she was severely emotionally and mentally abused, and she carried that weight alone. Without siblings to share the burden or offer solidarity, every word and every wound landed directly on her. The isolation of being an only child meant she had no one to reality-check her parents' cruelty, no one to remind her that she was not the problem.

She knew, with absolute clarity, who she did not want to be as a parent. She wanted to break free from the cruelty she had endured. But having my father as a partner forced her into the disciplinarian role, whether she wanted it or not. His reluctance to enforce rules left her carrying the obligation to create structure and represent authority, even though she had never been given healthy models for how to do so.

For my sisters and me, this meant sudden or random discipline mixed with permissiveness. I often thought of my mother as a ticking time-bomb, never knowing what would set her off. Some mornings she would come downstairs with a smile and a cheerful, "Good morning, Glory!" Other mornings, she would be yelling about something missing, accusing us of moving it, and the day would begin in chaos. Those swings were signals, cues that shaped how we learned to scan the emotional weather before we even entered a room.

Much later, I learned that she had been diagnosed with bipolar disorder, something she never told me directly. That silence shaped how we made sense of her inconsistency. We were left to piece together the reasons for her volatility on our own; children trying to decode adult storms without the language to name them.

I can see now that her inconsistency was not born of malice but of exhaustion, unhealed wounds, and untreated illness. She was trying to parent without a map, carrying the weight of her own trauma while also compensating for my father's absence in the role of boundary-setter. She wanted to love us differently than she had been loved, but the tools she had inherited were blunt and broken.

This is the conflict of the reluctant disciplinarian: She longed to be the safe harbor, but circumstance, history, and illness pushed her into the role of enforcer. And because she had never experienced healthy boundaries herself, she could rarely provide them for us.

Looking back at both of my parents, I can see how love and limitation lived side by side. My father's gentleness gave me warmth but not always safety. My mother's determination gave me structure but not always stability. Together, they carried the struggle so many families face: parents doing their best with the tools they were given, even when those tools were dull or damaged. Their behaviors, reactions, and silences were signals, shaping how we learned to navigate closeness, conflict, and uncertainty.

My parents' stories remind us that parenting is never simple. It is shaped by history, trauma, longing, and the desire to do better than what came before. And while every family's story is unique, the patterns are often familiar.

Before we move forward, I invite you to pause and consider your own inheritance.

SIGNALS FOR REFLECTION

- What were the most common phrases or "rules" you heard in your home while growing up? How did they make you feel at the time?
- If you had two parents or caregivers in your life, which one leaned more toward being the "fun" one, and which one leaned more toward being the "disciplinarian"? How did that dynamic shape your sense of safety or freedom?
- If you had one parent or caregiver in your life, did they lean more towards the "fun" side, or the "disciplinarian"? How did that dynamic shape your sense of safety or freedom?
- Did you ever feel caught between affection and authority, unsure where the boundaries truly were? How did that show up in your family of origin?
- Looking back, can you see the intentions behind your parents' choices, even when the outcomes were painful or inconsistent?
- If your parents modeled unhealthy childrearing patterns, in which ways do you notice yourself repeating those patterns? And in which ways have you consciously tried to break them?
- How do you hold compassion for the wounds your parents carried, while also acknowledging the impact those wounds had on you?

CLOSING THOUGHTS

Every family carries its own story, written both in love and in wounds. My parents longed to raise us differently than they had been raised, and in many ways they did. But they also carried forward patterns they never intended to repeat. That is the paradox of inheritance. We receive both the gifts our parents pass on and the gaps they cannot fill, even when those gaps were never part of their intention.

When we look back at our childhoods, it is easy to focus on what was missing or what hurt. Yet there is also power in recognizing the intentions behind the actions, even when the execution fell short. My father's longing to be loved, my mother's determination not to repeat cruelty, these were seeds of love, even if they sometimes grew into uneven fruit.

The truth is, none of us parent in a vacuum. We are shaped by what came before, and we shape what comes after. The question is not whether we will pass something on, but what we will choose to pass forward. Awareness is the first step in breaking cycles, and compassion for ourselves and for those who raised us is what allows us to begin again with intention.

My parents' stories were not isolated; they were part of a much larger pattern. To understand them fully, I had to step back and look at the wider evolution of parenting itself.

THE EVOLUTION OF PARENTING STYLES

From Obedience to Overprotection

THE AUTHORITARIAN NORM

During my childhood and even my teen years, I witnessed first-hand the style of parenting that had dominated civilization for centuries. In many of my friends' homes, the refrain was familiar: "Do what I say because I'm your parent." Often this was paired with: "Don't you dare make me look bad." This fear-driven, dominate-or-be-dominated approach—authoritarian parenting—has been the norm across cultures and generations, though certainly not by any child's choice. These phrases were signals, early cues about power, obedience, and where a child's voice fit in the family hierarchy.

Historically, authoritarian parenting grew out of a world-view where children were seen less as individuals and more as progeny—extensions of their parents, to be molded and controlled. For centuries, across many cultures, children were treated almost like property. A shoemaker's son was expected to become a shoemaker, a king's child was trained for rulership, and daughters were primarily confined to domestic roles. Autonomy was rarely considered; obedience was the expectation.

This legacy helps explain why authoritarian styles persisted for so long. Parents believed they had both the right and the duty to shape their children's paths, often without regard for the child's voice or individuality. While today we recognize the value of choice and emotional connection, echoes of that history still influence families who lean heavily on control. Those echoes show up in the signals that children receive about whose needs matter most and how safe it is to express themselves.

Understanding this history matters, because many parents who lean toward heavy control are not simply choosing it in isolation. They are echoing patterns that were passed down for generations. Recognizing that legacy can open the door to change.

Ironically, my own home, with its broken rules and unpredictable enforcement, became a safe harbor for many of my friends. Despite the chaos, the closeness and affection that lived in our house drew them in. They found comfort in the warmth, even when arguments erupted. For me, though, it left a yearning for more structure and consistency. Those longings were signals too, subtle indicators of what helped me feel grounded.

What I have come to realize in recent years is that there is a certain comfort in boundaries. Rules and guidelines provide a safety zone in a child's environment, allowing them to explore more freely within the confines of that zone. Without them, freedom can feel like instability.

Think of it like this: Imagine a friend invites you to play a game. You begin to play together when suddenly your friend interrupts: "Wait, here are some rules to follow." You adjust, only to have the rules change again a few minutes later. You never know if you will be rewarded or punished, praised or scolded. It becomes impossible to relax into the experience. Parenting without consistent boundaries can feel the same. Children read those shifting rules as signals about whether the world is predictable or precarious.

Parenting experts often talk about the difference between authoritarian and authoritative styles. Authoritarian parenting leans on control and fear, and research shows it can leave kids feeling anxious inside and less sure of their own choices. Of course, culture and personality play a role, but the overall pattern is pretty consistent. What's more, when authority is built on fear, it often spills into a "rules don't apply to me" mindset, where those in charge start believing they can cross boundaries without consequences. On the other hand, studies keep coming back to the same point: kids thrive when parents mix warmth with clear expectations. That balance does more than create obedience, it builds resilience. And often inconsistent boundaries reflect more than just parenting style, they can echo the way a parent was raised. If a childhood was marked by unpredictability or fear, those patterns may be repeated, even when a parent longs to do things differently. Those repetitions are signals, often passed down without awareness.

My own parents resisted authoritarianism because of their childhoods, yet they still struggled to find balance. I give them credit for recognizing that a fear-based approach was unacceptable. Their struggle wasn't about intention; it was about the patterns they had inherited and were still learning to unlearn. Research has confirmed what they sensed intuitively: consistently authoritarian parenting often leaves children more inwardly distressed and less confident in their choices, though context and individual differences also shape the outcome.

THE PENDULUM SWINGS

As many children of authoritarian households grew up and became parents themselves, a good number of them rejected that model outright. There was a dawning awareness that parents were not infallible, and that blind obedience was neither healthy nor sustainable. What followed was a wave of trial-and-error parenting, as mothers and fathers experimented with new approaches. These shifts were signals of a cultural awakening, a collective attempt to rewrite the messages children received about power and connection.

By the 1980s, many parents leaned into permissiveness, often saying things like, "I want to be my child's friend so they know they can trust me and tell me anything." Or "I want to encourage my child, not restrict them. I want them to feel like the sky's the limit." These desires came from love, but without boundaries, they left children unprepared for the realities of adulthood.

At the same time, the rise of twenty-four-hour news added a new layer of pressure. I remember the nightly broadcasts vividly, the announcer's sober reminder: "It's 10:00 p.m., do you know where your children are?" Those broadcasts made harmful incidents, which were dramatic but rare, feel constant and immediate. For many parents, vivid headlines amplified the sense of danger and nudged families toward more protective choices. Research on risk perception shows that sensational, memorable events shape how people judge danger. So, while headlines don't tell the whole story about actual probabilities, they do change what parents worry about and how they behave.

Widespread news coverage amplified dramatic stories, and parents understandably took them to heart. Many began restricting their children's access to the outside world. Playtime in the backyard or walks around the neighborhood came with a hovering parent watching every move, waiting for a stranger to appear with candy and a van. Most of the real risks our kids faced, like traffic injuries, were far more common than stranger abduction. But a dramatic headline stuck in people's minds, and suddenly the unlikely felt urgent. It's worth noticing which fears were stories and which were the evidence we actually needed to act on. The fear of "what if?" overrode reason, and the constant drumbeat of worst-case scenarios shaped a generation of anxious parenting. Those fears became signals, often teaching children that the world was more dangerous than it truly was.

From this mix of heightened societal fears and rising perfectionistic standards, the "helicopter parent" emerged, hovering, overprotective, unwilling to let children stumble or fail. In more recent years, the "bulldozer parent" has broken through, determined to clear every obstacle before a child even sees it. The result has been generations of children who struggle to adapt, and sometimes demand external "safe spaces" because they have not built internal ones.

Yes, there is value in protecting children. But there is also danger in overprotection. Life will not always give us warnings or soft landings. True resilience comes from learning to navigate bumps, not from having every bump removed. The balance lies in helping children build inner safe spaces—emotional security and coping mechanisms—so they can carry on even when the external world feels uncertain.

TRADITIONAL PARENTING STYLES

Over the last several decades, researchers have identified broad parenting styles that help us understand the patterns we inherit and the choices we make. No parent fits neatly into one category, but these frameworks give us language for what many of us have felt—the push and pull between love, fear, freedom, and control.

- **Authoritarian:** High control, low warmth. Authoritarian parenting often creates compliance in the short term, but at a cost. Children raised in this environment may learn to follow rules, yet struggle with internal motivation, because their behavior is driven by fear rather than understanding. Many become hyper-vigilant, scanning for tone, posture, or mood shifts to avoid punishment. Others rebel quietly, learning to hide mistakes instead of learning from them. The emotional signal they receive is clear: "Your worth depends on obedience." This can shape how they approach authority, conflict, and self-expression well into adulthood.
- **Permissive:** High warmth, low control. Permissive parenting often comes from a place of deep love and a desire to avoid the harshness parents once experienced themselves. But without consistent boundaries, children may struggle to develop frustration tolerance, emotional regulation, or a sense of accountability. They often become overwhelmed by choices they are not developmentally ready to make. The signal they receive is confusing: "You are free, but you are also on your own." This can lead to anxiety, entitlement, or difficulty navigating environments where limits are necessary.
- **Authoritative:** High warmth, high control. Authoritative parenting blends warmth with structure, offering children both emotional safety and clear expectations. Parents who use this style set boundaries with consistency, but they also explain the "why" behind their decisions, inviting dialogue rather than demanding obedience. Children raised in

authoritative homes tend to develop strong internal regulation because they experience limits as guidance rather than control. The signal they receive is steady and empowering: "You are capable, and I am here to support you as you grow." This balance of connection and accountability becomes the foundation for emotional security, resilience, and healthy autonomy. Research consistently shows this style fosters confidence and secure attachment. It is often described as the "sweet spot" between love and limits.

- **Gentle Parenting:** High empathy, high guidance. Parents lead with respect, modeling calm communication and emotional awareness. Discipline is not about punishment but about teaching, guiding, and repairing. Children raised in this style often feel deeply seen and valued, learning to trust both their own emotions and the steady presence of their caregivers. The risk, however, is that without clear boundaries, empathy can slide into permissiveness. At its best, gentle parenting blends compassion with consistency, helping children grow resilient while knowing they are loved unconditionally.

- **Neglectful or uninvolved:** Low warmth, low control. Neglectful parenting is not always intentional; it can stem from burnout, trauma, mental health challenges, or lack of support. But regardless of the cause, the impact on children is profound. Without emotional or physical presence, children learn to meet their own needs prematurely, often becoming overly independent or emotionally shut down. The signal they internalize is painful: "Your needs are too much." This can shape attachment and self-worth issues, and difficulties with the ability to trust others long into adulthood.

Beyond these four, cultural shifts have given rise to newer labels:

- **Helicopter parenting:** Helicopter parenting is rooted in fear and the desire to protect, yet it unintentionally communicates a lack of trust in the child's abilities. When parents hover, fix, or intervene too quickly, children lose opportunities to build resilience, problem-solving skills, and confidence. The signal they receive is subtle but powerful: "You cannot handle this without me." Over time, this can lead to dependence, anxiety, or avoidance of challenges because the child has not had the chance to experience manageable struggle.
- **Bulldozer parenting:** Bulldozer parenting takes protection a step further by removing obstacles before the child ever encounters them. While the intention is loving, the long-term impact is limiting. Children raised this way may struggle with perseverance, emotional regulation, or the ability to tolerate discomfort. They may expect the world to adjust for them because that has been their lived experience. The signal they receive is: "The world is too hard for you, so I must clear the path." This can undermine their sense of agency and resilience.

Each of these styles comes from somewhere—often from love, sometimes from fear, and usually from the desire to do better than the generation before. But without balance, even the most well-intentioned approach can leave children with gaps. Too much control and they lose their voice, too much freedom and they lose their footing. The signals children receive from these patterns shape how they learn to navigate autonomy, safety, and connection.

Understanding these styles helps us see the spectrum of parenting approaches—from too much control to too little, from fear to indulgence. But naming the styles is only the beginning. What matters most is how children actually experience them. And what I have come to realize, both in my own life and in decades of work with families, is that beneath all the labels there is one essential truth: Children find comfort in boundaries.

THE COMFORT OF BOUNDARIES

It is simple and human to find comfort in boundaries. Rules and guidelines, when sensible and consistent, feel like safety zones that let children run, play, and test themselves without constant fear. Broad research and my own experience both point to the same idea: Predictability wrapped in care tends to encourage safe exploration.

Think of it like starting a new job. If no one explains your responsibilities, or if the rules keep shifting from day to day, it becomes impossible to acclimate to the work. You are always bracing for the next correction, scanning for what you might have missed, unsure of how success will even be measured. Parenting without consistent boundaries feels the same. Children may appear free, but inside they are unsettled, always wondering when the rules will change and how harshly the consequences will fall. Those internal calculations are signals, shaping how they learn to anticipate, adapt, and protect themselves.

My parents rejected the harshness they grew up with, but rejecting fear is not the same as knowing how to build something healthier. They were trying to parent differently without having ever seen what "different" looked like.

Studies tend to point to the same thing. Kids do best when parents combine warmth with clear, consistent limits—the "authoritative approach"—but culture and individual temperament change how that looks in practice. Children raised in fear may comply outwardly, but inwardly they learn to hide and suppress their emotions and to disconnect from their own needs. Boundaries without love create obedience, but not resilience. They can become harmful when they're rigid, punitive, or out of step with a family's culture.

What truly helps are steady limits wrapped in warmth and clear explanation. They create safety. They give children the confidence to take risks and make mistakes, knowing that even when they stumble, the ground beneath them will hold.

We will explore boundaries more deeply in Chapter 8, taking a closer look at how the limits we set become signals of safety, trust, and connection.

FINDING BALANCE

I know this may sound critical, but my point is not to shame. Every parenting style comes from love, fear, or both. Parents want to protect and encourage their children, to do better than the previous generation. The problem is not intention; it is imbalance.

Children need both freedom and boundaries. They need their parents to be parents, not peers. They need external safety nets while they build the internal ones that will carry them into adulthood. Without freedom, they cannot grow. Without boundaries, they cannot feel safe.

Balance is not a static point; it is a living practice. Some days it leans more toward structure, other days toward flexibility. What matters is not perfection, but consistency and repair. Repair means returning to connection after a rupture, naming what went wrong, taking responsibility, and reestablishing safety with warmth and clear boundaries. When parents can admit mistakes, reset boundaries, and return to connection, children learn one of the most vital lessons of all—that relationships can bend without breaking. Those moments of repair are signals, showing children that conflict does not end connection.

True resilience comes not from never falling, but from learning how to rise again after a fall. It means learning that it's okay to take risks, even if you don't succeed—and that success is not the measure of everything. Children rise best when they know two things are always true: that they are loved, and that the ground beneath them is steady enough to hold them as they try again.

Parenting has never been about choosing the "perfect" style or avoiding mistakes altogether. It is about learning, adjusting, and repairing as we go. Each generation swings between extremes, trying to correct what came before. The real work is not in the swing; it is in the steady middle ground we create for our children day by day.

Before I close this chapter, I invite you to pause and reflect. The following "Signals" are not about judgment, but about awareness. They are a chance to notice where you may lean too far toward freedom, where you may lean too far toward control, and where balance is beginning to take root.

SIGNALS FOR REFLECTION

- Which of the cultural messages about parenting (obedience, permissiveness, helicoptering, bulldozing) feels most familiar from your community or generation?
- In your own parenting, where do you notice yourself leaning

more toward control, and where do you lean more toward freedom?

- How do you balance empathy with guidance, so your children see both your compassion and your consistency?
- How do media, cultural narratives, or community expectations influence the way you set boundaries?
- What boundaries in your home feel steady and consistent, and where do you sense instability or unpredictability?
- How do you model repair when you make mistakes? Do your children see you acknowledge, reset, and reconnect?
- Where in your family life do you see resilience being built, and where might overprotection or inconsistency be getting in the way?

CLOSING THOUGHTS

Parenting has always evolved in response to what came before. Each generation tries to correct the mistakes of the last. But swinging too far in either direction, too rigid or too permissive, leaves children unprepared for the road of life.

The path forward is not about choosing one style over another. It is about creating balance: setting boundaries that provide safety, paired with love that provides security. That balance is what allows children to explore, grow, and eventually stand on their own.

And in the end, that balance becomes part of the legacy we leave behind—not just in how our children live, but in how they carry forward the lessons of safety, love, and resilience into the generations that follow.

As we turn from the broad sweep of parenting styles to the more intimate realities of family life, we will see how balance, boundaries, and love are tested most deeply in moments of loss, and how the secure attachments we build become the anchors our children carry forward.

"YARONA, DO YOU REALIZE THAT WE'RE ORPHANS NOW?"

The Final Threads of Life

After our mother died, my sister Mori and I were talking on the phone. During a pause she said softly, "Yarona, do you realize that we're orphans now?"

My breath whooshed out of me. My chest constricted. I could not speak.

In that moment, we both realized that the final threads of physical connection we had to our parents were truly gone. I could no longer pick up the phone to call either my mother or my father, who had passed just a few years before her. I could not send them a random message about something silly that happened or share a passing thought. I could not pop over to their house for a hug, a smile of reassurance, or a helping hand.

The absence was stark. The finality, undeniable.

It was one of those moments when the signals of loss arrive

all at once, not through words but through the sudden quiet where connection used to be.

THE MOMENT EVERYTHING CHANGED

That realization became heartbreakingly real when I was pregnant with my son. My husband and I had taken a brief trip to Arizona, one of my mom's favorite places. She loved the vast desert landscape, so different from New Jersey where she had lived most of her life.

I was five months pregnant, exhausted from travel and from pregnancy itself. On autopilot after the long plane ride, I stared out the window as palm trees blurred past. Without thinking, I turned to my husband, Carl, and said, "Oh! I have to call my mother and send her a picture of the palm trees. She'll be so jealous we're here."

The words left my mouth before my mind caught up. And then the silence hit.

THE WEIGHT OF ABSENCE AND THE POWER OF MEMORY

As my laughter faded into painful awareness and I fell silent, my husband looked at me briefly before turning back to the road. He had no words, and neither did I. Pain stole them as my mind went blank and all I could do was feel. I could not believe I had forgotten. I could not fathom that moment without her. And the knowledge that I could not just call her and make a silly, gleeful observation or a passing comment and get her response washed over me and brought a wave of heartbreak with it in that instant.

Whether she would have responded the same way she had countless times before, or whether her words would have been unique to that particular situation, I knew I would never get her real-time perspective again. That is the sharp edge of grief: realizing that the unfolding dialogue between us has ended.

Sometimes we think we know exactly what someone will say, but the truth is that people surprise us. Even those we know best carry depths we will never fully uncover. What I realized in that moment was that I would never again be surprised by my mother. That was the absence I felt most deeply, not just her voice, but the possibility of discovering new layers of her heart and mind.

And yet, that realization also illuminated something else. While the physical connection was gone, the emotional, heart-centered connection remained. The relationship we had built over a lifetime did not vanish with her last breath. Our connection lives on in me, in the way I carry her lessons, in the way I mother my own child, and in the way her presence still surfaces in unexpected moments. Those moments are signals, quiet reminders that love continues to speak even when the person is no longer here to say the words.

WHAT LOSS TEACHES US ABOUT LOVE AND SECURITY

When you have truly known someone, the thread of that connection remains. How it shows up changes, but it can continue to shape us. It may be cut by time, distance, or even death, but for many of us, the mark that person leaves on our hearts often endures.

Loss teaches us that we can never be fully prepared. Each loss is unique, as unique as the person themselves. But loss also teaches us what matters most.

As a parent now, I understand this in a new way. When my final moments come, I know the one thing I will want is certainty that my child will be OK without me. Not just physically or financially, but emotionally. That he will carry me in his heart, and that the security of our bond will steady him even when I am gone.

This is the gift we aim to give our children: emotional security. The knowledge that love does not end when life does. These are the signals that matter most, the ones that tell a child they are held even when they cannot see us.

A CONVERSATION WITH MY SON

When my son was four, and frustrated that I wouldn't put his shoes on for him, I gently said, "Connor, you know, one day Mommy and Daddy will not be here anymore, that's one of the reasons you have to do these things for yourself."

We sat together for a moment, letting the words settle. Then I asked softly, "How will you feel when Mommy and Daddy are no longer here?"

He looked at me with a calm certainty that surprised me. Then he pointed to his chest and said, "I'll be ok Mommy, because you will always be here, in my heart."

The simplicity of his answer took my breath away. In that instant, I felt both the ache of truth and the gift of reassurance. He was not denying loss. He was showing me that he already understood something many adults struggle to grasp: that love and connection do not end when life does. In that moment, I knew he was absorbing the message I wanted him to carry. His words were a signal back to me, a reflection of the emotional safety he had already internalized.

Each day he is learning to find emotional security, not in the illusion that nothing will ever change, but in the deeper truth that the bonds we build live on inside us.

THE MARKS THEY LEAVE BEHIND

Grief has also taught me to notice the ways my parents live on in me. Sometimes it is in the big things, sometimes it's in the smallest details.

When Connor was an infant, I remember holding him and suddenly noticing the veiny bumps on the backs of my hands, the curve of my palms, the shape of my fingers. For a moment, I saw my mother's hands instead of my own.

The gut punch of grief was immediate. But then came the deep well of comfort: Here was a tangible reminder that she was still with me. Her mark lived on in me, and as I held my son, I felt that continuity passing forward. It was the sense that her presence was imprinted not only on me, but carried into the next generation. These quiet recognitions are signals, the kind that surface without warning and remind us of the threads that endure.

SIGNALS FOR REFLECTION

Take a moment to think about the connections in your life that have come and gone, whether through death, distance, or choice. Ask yourself:

- What did those connections teach me?
- Of the connections that mattered most, how can I keep them alive to pass on to my children?
- How can I carry the lessons I have learned from those I have lost and pass them down for deeper learning?

A deeper thought to ponder: As a parent, what is the one thing you want to know before you leave this world?

If your answer is, "That my children will be OK without me," then you must start with that end goal in mind.

CLOSING THOUGHTS

Loss strips life down to its essentials. It reminds us that what endures is not the physical presence of those we love, but the emotional security we built with them. That security becomes the anchor we carry forward, the quiet assurance that love does not end when life does.

As parents, this is the legacy we are shaping every day. Not just the routines, the lessons, or the milestones, but the deep sense of safety and belonging our children will carry long after we are gone. When my son pressed his hand to his chest and told me I would always be in his heart, I realized he was already learning the truth I most wanted him to know: that love endures beyond presence, and when it is paired with secure attachment, it becomes the thread that binds us across time, distance, and even death.

This is the gift we can give our children, the knowledge that they are never truly alone, that love is a constant presence they can draw on in moments of fear, loss, or uncertainty. It is not only their anchor in times of loss, it is also the beginning of the legacy we leave behind.

In the next chapter, we will shift from the personal to the developmental. We will look at the critical childhood years and the five domains of growth that shape who our children become. Just as love and secure attachment form a foundation for resilience in the face of loss, these domains give us a map of the signals our children send every day.

By learning to see beneath the surface, to notice not only what is spoken but also what is unspoken, we can respond with clarity, compassion, and confidence.

CHAPTER 4

THE FIVE DOMAINS OF DEVELOPMENT

How Your Child's Growth Shows Up Through Everyday Signals

UNDERSTANDING YOUR CHILD'S GROWTH THROUGH THE SIGNALS THEY SEND

Every child grows in ways we can see and in ways we can only feel. Some of their growth shows up in milestones like learning to walk or forming sentences. Much of it shows up in subtler moments. A sudden clinginess. A burst of independence. A meltdown that seems to come out of nowhere.

These moments are not random. They are signals. Signals about what your child is working on internally. Signals about what feels hard, exciting, overwhelming, or brand new.

When we understand the five core domains of development, we are not memorizing science. We are learning how to read the cues our children are already giving us. And when we can read those cues, we can respond with more clarity, more compassion, and more confidence.

You do not need to become an expert in child development. You simply need a gentle way to understand what your child's behavior might be trying to tell you. That is the purpose of this chapter.

THE MORNING EVERYTHING FELT HARD

When my son was about four, we had a morning that felt like it unraveled before it even began. He woke up tired and cranky. His farina was too lumpy. His pants were too tight. The tag on his shirt was "itchy." The zipper on his jacket would not cooperate. By the time we reached the front door, he was in tears, and I was holding back my own.

At the time, it felt like everything was falling apart over nothing. But later that night, when I replayed the day in my mind, I realized something important. Every one of those moments was a signal. His body was tired. His senses were overwhelmed. His emotions were close to the surface. His skills were still developing. He was not giving me a hard time. He was **having** a hard time.

That morning, and other mornings like it, have taught me something I have carried with me ever since. When we understand what our children are working on developmentally, their behavior becomes less confusing and we become more compassionate. We stop seeing defiance and start seeing communication. We stop seeing drama and start seeing signals.

THE FIVE DOMAINS OF DEVELOPMENT

Each domain below is intentionally simple and parent-friendly. Think of them as lenses that help you understand what your child may be signaling at any given moment.

1. PHYSICAL DEVELOPMENT

Physical development is about how children use and understand their bodies. This includes balance, coordination, strength, and the small movements that help them manage everyday tasks. When something is physically hard, children often communicate it through frustration, avoidance, or sudden "I can't" moments.

Example: Your child throws their shoes across the room when asked to put them on. It looks like defiance, but tying laces or managing stiff sneakers may still feel too hard.

Signal Interpretation: *"My body is still learning this. I need patience and support, but I also need practice so I can grow."*

2. COGNITIVE DEVELOPMENT

Cognitive development is how children think, explore, and make sense of the world. It includes curiosity, problem solving, imagination, and the desire to test ideas. When their minds are growing quickly, children often experiment in ways that look messy or mischievous.

Example: Your child pours water from cup to cup until it spills everywhere. They are not trying to create chaos. They are learning about volume, control, cause and effect.

Signal Interpretation: *"I am trying to understand how things work. Please guide me so my curiosity is encouraged, but does not turn into chaos."*

3. LANGUAGE DEVELOPMENT

Language development includes both what children understand and what they can express. When their feelings grow faster than their words, behavior becomes their primary form of communication. This is often where big reactions show up.

Example: Your toddler screams because you gave them the blue cup instead of the red one. They are not being dramatic. They simply do not have the words yet to explain their disappointment or preference.

Signal Interpretation: *"My feelings are bigger than my words right now. Help me name them and show me how to express them respectfully."*

4. SOCIAL AND EMOTIONAL DEVELOPMENT

Social and emotional development is how children learn to understand themselves and others. It includes sharing, taking turns, reading cues, expressing feelings, managing frustration, building empathy, and forming relationships. These skills grow slowly and unevenly, which means children often communicate their needs through behavior long before they can explain what is happening inside them.

Example: Your child grabs a toy from another child and then bursts into tears when asked to give it back. They are not trying to be rude or dramatic. They are practicing boundaries, communication, and emotional regulation all at once.

Signal Interpretation: *"I am learning how to be with others and how to manage my feelings. Stay close and help me learn what is okay and what is not."*

5. ADAPTIVE AND SELF-HELP SKILLS

Adaptive skills are the everyday abilities that help children take care of themselves and move through the world with growing independence. This includes feeding, dressing, toileting, cleaning up, following routines, and managing simple responsibilities. When these skills are still developing, children often show resistance, avoidance, or sudden "I can't" moments, especially when they feel rushed or overwhelmed.

Example: Your child refuses to put on their jacket even though they have done it many times before. They are not being lazy. They may be tired, overstimulated, or need more time to practice a skill that still feels new.

Signal Interpretation: *"I want to do things on my own, but I still need support and structure. Please give me space to try and boundaries to keep me steady."*

SIGNALS FOR REFLECTION

Take a moment to pause and check in with yourself. These questions are not meant to judge your parenting. They are simply invitations to notice the signals in your home and in your relationship with your child.

- When your child struggles with a task, what signals do you notice in their body, their tone, or their behavior?
- How do you usually respond when your child's frustration or overwhelm shows up suddenly?
- Which moments in the day feel the hardest for your child, and what might those moments be signaling about their developmental needs?
- When your child experiments, explores, or makes a mess,

what signals are they sending about their curiosity or problem solving?

- How do you feel when your child cannot express themselves with words and uses behavior instead? What signals do you notice in yourself in those moments?
- Which social situations seem to challenge your child the most, and what might those challenges be communicating about their skills or comfort level?
- When your child has a big emotional reaction, what do you think their feelings are trying to tell you?
- What signals do you send to your child when you are tired, stressed, or overwhelmed? How do you imagine they interpret those signals?
- Looking back at your own childhood, what signals did you learn to send or suppress? How might those early experiences shape the way you respond to your child now?
- Which domain feels easiest for you to support, and which ones feel more challenging? What might help you feel more confident in the harder moments?

CLOSING THOUGHTS

When we look at development through the lens of signals, everything becomes easier to understand. A meltdown becomes a message. A refusal becomes a clue. A clingy moment becomes a request for safety. These signals help us see the child beneath the behavior, which is essential for connection.

But understanding development does not mean excusing every behavior or stepping back from our role as leaders. Children grow best when they feel both understood and guided. They need room to practice new skills, and they also need the steady presence of a parent who can hold boundaries while staying attuned to what is happening beneath the surface.

It is very easy, especially when we are tired or overwhelmed, to project our adult expectations onto our children. We forget how much they are still learning. We forget how much of their world is brand new. Awareness is what helps us pause before reacting, so we can respond to the child in front of us rather than the adult we expect them to be.

As you move forward, hold this balance gently. Notice the signals. Stay curious. And remember that your child's development is not an excuse for behavior, but a context that helps you respond with clarity, compassion, and leadership. Every behavior is a signal, and every signal is an invitation to guide your child with both understanding and strength.

CHAPTER 5

THE 3 C'S OF EMOTIONALLY SECURE PARENTING

Connection, Control, and Competency: The Signals That Shape How Children Grow

UNDERSTANDING WHAT CHILDREN NEED BENEATH THEIR SIGNALS

In the previous chapter, we explored the five domains of development and the signals children send as they grow. Understanding those signals helps us see the child beneath the behavior. But knowing what a child is working on internally is only half of the picture. The other half is how we respond.

Children do not grow in isolation. They grow in relationship with us. The way we respond to their signals becomes a signal of its own. Our tone, our presence, our boundaries, our patience, our frustration, and our encouragement all communicate something long before we say a word.

This is where the 3 C's come in.

Before a child can feel competent or exercise healthy control, they must first feel connected. Connection is the soil from which all other growth emerges. It is the foundation that allows children to explore, take risks, make mistakes, and try again. When connection is strong, children feel safe enough to learn. When it is weak, everything else becomes harder.

The 3 C's, connection, control, and competency, are the three psychological needs that support healthy development. They are rooted in the Self Determination Theory developed by psychologists Richard Ryan and Edward Deci, which explains that all humans share three basic needs: relatedness, autonomy, and competence. When these needs are supported, children thrive. When they are ignored, children struggle.

I translate these needs into language that parents can use every day: Connection. Control. Competency.

Each of these needs shows up as a signal. Children signal when they feel disconnected. They signal when they feel powerless. They signal when they feel unsure of themselves. They also signal when these needs are met.

When we learn to read these signals, we can respond in ways that strengthen trust, reduce power struggles, and support emotional security.

THE 3 C'S IN ACTION

My staff once worked with a little boy named Mateo who was three years old and struggling with tantrums that seemed to erupt out of nowhere. His parents were exhausted. They had tried sticker charts, timeouts, taking away toys, and every strategy they could find online. Nothing worked.

When my team observed him at home, they noticed something important. Every time Mateo tried to do something for himself, pour his own juice, put on his shoes, choose a toy, his parents jumped in quickly. They were loving and well intentioned, but they were so eager to help that they unintentionally sent a signal that said, "We do not trust you to do this."

Mateo sent a signal back through tantrums, frustration, and refusal.

One afternoon, a staff member suggested a small shift. Instead of pouring his juice for him, they handed him a small pitcher and said, "Would you like to pour it yourself, or would you like me to help?"

His eyes lit up. He chose to pour it himself.

The first time, he spilled. His parents rushed forward, ready to fix it, but the staff member gently encouraged them to pause. Mateo steadied the pitcher, concentrated, and this time got most of the juice into the cup. The grin on his face said everything.

In that moment, all 3 C's were present, and each one was communicated through signals.

Connection: His parents stayed close, encouraging him without shaming him for the spill. *Signal sent: "You are safe with me."*

Control: He had a real choice and the freedom to act. *Signal sent: "Your voice matters."*

Competency: He experienced success, however small, and felt capable. *Signal sent: "You can do this."*

Over the next few weeks, as Mateo's parents began making these shifts in their daily routine, the tantrums began to fade. Not because the problem disappeared, but because his needs were finally being met. He felt seen. He felt some control. He felt capable. His behavior shifted because the signals in his environment shifted.

Children do not throw tantrums because they are bad. They throw tantrums because something essential is missing. When we meet their needs for connection, control, and competency, we give them the foundation to regulate themselves, to trust us, and to trust their own abilities.

These needs do not go away with age. They are the same needs that drive us as adults. We want to feel loved. We want to feel some control over our lives. We want to feel competent in what we do. When you give your child these three gifts early, you are not just shaping their childhood. You are shaping the way they will approach relationships, challenges, and opportunities for the rest of their lives.

Research confirms what many of us know intuitively. When these three needs are supported, children become more independent, more resilient, and more likely to maintain healthy behaviors. They also feel better about themselves and about their relationships with others.

Since this chapter introduces the 3 C's as a whole, there are no **Signals for Reflection** here. You'll find them in the next three chapters, where each C is explored one at a time.

CLOSING THOUGHTS

The 3 C's are not techniques or quick fixes. They are core human needs, and every need comes with a signal. When children feel disconnected, powerless, or unsure of themselves, they show us. When they feel safe, capable, and trusted, they show us that too. Their behavior is always communicating something, even when the message is hard to hear.

Our job is not to get it right every time. Our job is to stay aware. To pause long enough to notice the signals beneath the behavior. To remember that our responses become signals of their own. And to hold the balance between compassion and leadership as our children grow.

When we respond with connection, we send a signal that says, "You matter." When we offer healthy control, we send a signal that says, "Your voice has value." When we support competency, we send a signal that says, "You can do this."

These signals shape the way children see themselves and the world around them. They also shape the way they learn to communicate their needs, manage their emotions, and trust others.

As we move into the next chapter, we begin with the first and most essential of the 3 C's: connection. Children give us small clues about what strengthens their sense of safety and belonging. Understanding those clues is what prepares us to support their connection, autonomy, and competency.

Connection is the foundation of emotional security. It is the place where trust is built, where regulation begins, and where children learn that they do not have to face the world alone. It is also the lens that helps us understand what our children are trying to communicate beneath the surface.

This is where our deeper journey begins.

CHAPTER 6

THE NEED TO BOND

The First C: Connection

THE FIRST C: THE FOUNDATION OF EMOTIONAL SECURITY

Connection is the starting point for everything that follows in a child's development. It is the emotional anchor that helps children feel safe enough to explore, learn, take risks, and recover from mistakes. When children feel connected, their nervous systems settle. Their behavior softens. Their capacity to listen, cooperate, and regulate expands. When connection is shaky, everything else becomes harder.

Children communicate their need for connection through signals. Some of these signals are clear, like reaching for us, asking for help, or wanting to be held. Others are quieter and easier to miss. A sudden clinginess. A shift in tone. A meltdown at the end of a long day. Even defiance can be a signal that says, "I feel overwhelmed," or "I need you close, even if I cannot ask for it."

As adults, it is easy to misread these signals or interpret

them through the lens of our own stress, expectations, or upbringing. We may see a child's behavior as disrespectful or dramatic when, underneath, they are really signaling a need for reassurance or connection. When we slow down enough to notice these cues, we can respond in ways that strengthen the relationship rather than escalate the moment.

Connection is not about being perfect or endlessly patient. It is about being present. It is about sending our own signals back to our children that say, "You matter," "You are safe with me," and "I am here." These signals shape the way children see themselves and the world around them. They also shape the way they learn to communicate their needs, manage their emotions, and trust others.

CONNECTION: THE FIRST SURVIVAL INSTINCT

Most parents are hit with a life-changing realization the instant they first connect with their child. Whether born from you or not, the moment you are given the responsibility of raising another human into adulthood can be one of the most awe-filled and fear-inducing moments of your life.

I remember bringing Connor home from the hospital after five exhausting days of recovery from my emergency C-section. It was late at night and, as I tried to settle him into his bassinet, he began to cry. It was that terrifying, helpless infant cry. I couldn't soothe him, and I began to spiral.

He was beautiful, and I was terrified. What if I wasn't good enough? What if I messed him up? In that moment, I didn't believe my son could thrive with me as his mother.

That moment of despair was also a moment of truth. Connection is the first survival instinct. It is the foundation of everything else. As Deci and Ryan describe in their Self Determination Theory, it is the need to feel connected and to belong. Even in those early days, Connor was sending signals that said, "Stay close. I need you," and I was just learning how to read them.

Countless studies affirm this: People who feel seen, heard, and valued thrive. Social connection improves mental health, reduces stress, strengthens immunity, and even increases life expectancy. Isolation, on the other hand, has been linked to heart disease, stroke, and weakened immune systems. The COVID-19 pandemic gave us real-time evidence of how devastating disconnection can be.

From the very beginning, connection is not optional. It is survival.

CHILDREN AND DEVICES DO NOT MIX

Infants are born helpless, relying on others to meet their needs. Their first language of connection is crying, a signal that says, "I need you." Over time, they connect through their senses: sight, sound, touch, taste, and smell. They watch our faces, mimic our expressions, and learn through observation. These early exchanges are the building blocks of how children learn to read and send signals of their own.

But what happens when a screen interrupts that process?

I once met with a mother whose toddler could scroll a phone better than she could. At first, she saw this as a sign of intelligence, evidence that he was advanced for his age. But when she and I sat together, our conversation revealed something deeper: how screens can interrupt the most essential form of learning: human connection.

As she pulled out her phone and showed me thousands of videos, her pride was palpable. "Look how smart he is," she said. "He knows exactly how to find his shows. He can swipe, tap, even close ads. Isn't that amazing?"

Then her voice softened. "But I don't understand why he doesn't look at me when I talk to him. Why he'd rather watch the tablet than play with me. I don't understand why he has a developmental delay."

I could hear the ache in her words. She wasn't neglectful. She was devoted. She had been with him since the moment of his birth. She gave him the phone during diaper changes, at mealtimes, in the car, while shopping. Not because she didn't care, but because she was trying to cope. She thought she was keeping him happy, occupied, and stimulated.

What she didn't realize was that the very tool she believed was helping was also disrupting the back-and-forth signals her son needed to learn how to connect.

I explained gently: "When you hold up the phone to record him, you see his face through the screen. But he only sees the phone. He doesn't see your eyes. He doesn't see your smile or facial expressions. He hears your voice, but it's disembodied, coming from behind a rectangle. And because his vision is still limited, he cannot see around the phone to find you. For him, it's like being in solitary confinement, cut off from the very cues that teach him how to connect."

She looked at me, stunned. "I never thought of it that way," she whispered.

This is the hidden cost of screens in early childhood. Babies and toddlers learn connection through sight, sound, touch, and mimicry. They study our facial expressions, our tone, our gestures. When a device interrupts that, they lose access to the very human signals that wire their brains for belonging.

This mother wasn't failing her child. She was doing what so many of us do: leaning on the tools our culture normalizes, without realizing the developmental trade-offs. Once she understood, she began to shift. She started putting the phone down during meals, making eye contact during diaper changes, and saving videos for special moments rather than daily ones.

And slowly, she began to notice something: Her son started looking back at her. His signals were changing, because hers were too.

CREATE MOMENTS TO GENUINELY CONNECT

Connection requires presence. It requires us to put down the phone, look into our child's eyes, and let them know: You matter more than this screen.

When we put a phone between ourselves and our infants, it is not just a distraction. For them, it is a kind of isolation. Babies have a limited range of sight. They cannot see around the phone. They cannot reach for our face. They cannot make eye contact or read our expressions. All they get is a glowing rectangle and a voice that feels distant.

If screens regularly sit between us and babies during core caregiving moments, research and clinical experience suggest that those devices can become preferred sources of attention, reducing face-to-face learning opportunities. And because children learn through unspoken signals, they will quickly absorb the message that the screen is more important than they are.

But when we put the phone down, when we let them see our eyes, our smiles, our full presence, we send the opposite message: You are worth my attention. You are worth my time. You are worth my connection.

PLAY: THE "NOT SO SECRET" KEY TO CONNECTION

From the very beginning, exploration is the way humans learn. Long before formal education, before words, before rules, children discover their environment by touching, tasting, crawling, climbing, and experimenting. Exploration is play, and play is connection.

When a baby drops a spoon from the high chair and watches you pick it up again and again, they are not trying to annoy you. They are studying cause and effect. They are learning: I can act on the world, and the world responds. That is the seed of both autonomy and connection. It is also a signal that says, "Stay with me. Notice what I'm discovering."

Play is the laboratory of curiosity. It is how children test boundaries, discover patterns, and begin to understand themselves in relation to others. Through play, they learn:

- **Social rules:** taking turns, sharing, and negotiating
- **Emotional regulation:** feeling joy, frustration, disappointment, and repair
- **Problem-solving:** experimenting, failing, and trying again
- **Belonging:** realizing that laughter, imagination, and shared activity create bonds

When we join children in play, we are saying: "I am curious about your world. I want to see how you see." That act of shared curiosity is one of the deepest forms of connection. It is also one of the clearest signals we can send that says, "You matter to me."

I grew up with board games, and those games became more than entertainment. They were windows into personality, into dreams, into the quirks of the people I loved. My brother Danny's obsession with Monopoly revealed his fierce competitiveness and his playful stubbornness. Even as an adult, that part of him remained. When illness finally dulled his drive to finish a game, I knew something had shifted. Play had always been the place where I knew him best.

With Connor, play has become a mirror of his perfectionist streak. He hates losing, and at first, when he lost a game, I wanted to smooth it over, to tell him it didn't matter. But I realized play was giving him something more important than victory: it was giving him the chance to practice disappointment, to feel frustration, and to learn resilience. By sitting with him in those moments, by naming his feelings and helping him find strategies, we weren't just playing a game. We were building tools for life. And the signals I sent in those moments—calm, presence, belief in him—were shaping how he learned to handle challenges.

Play is also the first way children learn about their environment. A toddler stacking blocks is learning about balance and gravity. A child digging in the dirt is learning about texture, cause and effect, and the joy of discovery. These are not trivial activities. They form the foundation of scientific thinking, emotional intelligence, and social connection.

And here is the key: play is not just for children. When we allow ourselves to play with them, to be silly, to imagine and explore, we reconnect with our own curiosity. We show them that learning is not something that ends with adulthood. It is a lifelong practice of wonder.

So when we play, we are not just passing time. We are saying: "I see you. I delight in you. I want to explore this world with you." And that message, more than any toy or game, is what creates a lasting bond.

A SNOW DAY LESSON IN CONNECTION

Connection is not only built in moments of joy and play. Sometimes it is built most deeply in moments of repair.

When Connor was in preschool, we had an emergency delayed opening for his school. That morning, I had a doctor's appointment and a full schedule, and the day quickly went sideways. I was rushed, frustrated, and already feeling behind.

When we finally arrived and parked, we had to walk two blocks in the snow to get to the building. And what does any four-year-old want to do in the snow? Of course, he wanted to play.

As Connor began stomping and laughing, I grew more impatient. I tried to hurry him along, urging, "Connor, come on, we've got to go now." In the rush, he slipped down onto his knees in the snow. I quickly brushed him off and kept moving, still focused on getting him inside.

Once he was safely in the building, the moment stayed with me. All day I replayed it in my mind, asking myself what I needed to do about it. By the time I picked him up from school, I knew the answer: I needed to apologize.

So in the car I said, "Connor, I need to apologize. This morning when we got to school and you wanted to play in the snow, I shouldn't have rushed you like I did, causing you to fall. I should have said, 'I see that you want to play in the snow, but now is not the time. We have to get into school quickly, and later, when I pick you up, we can definitely play in the snow then.' I'm sorry for that."

There was a pause. Then from the back seat came his quiet but steady reply: "Mommy, I accept your apology."

That moment was a gift. It reminded me that connection is not about being perfect. It is about being present, being honest, and owning our mistakes. When we apologize to our children, we model accountability. We show them that adults make mistakes too, and that repair is always possible. And in doing so, we send a powerful signal: "Our relationship is stronger than this moment."

CONNECTION WITH OLDER CHILDREN AND TEENS

Connection does not stop when our children outgrow our laps. In fact, it becomes even more vital as they move into adolescence. However, the ways in which they seek connection shift, creating new challenges. Whereas a toddler runs into your arms, a teenager may roll their eyes. While a child begs for your attention, a teen may retreat behind a closed door. But the need underneath is the same: "See me, hear me, value me."

Adolescence is a time of individuation. Teens are practicing separation, but they are not rejecting connection. They are testing whether the bond can stretch without breaking. This is where many parents misinterpret distance as disinterest. In reality, teens need us to stay present without pushing, remaining available without smothering.

Connection with older children often looks quieter, less obvious:

- Sitting side by side in the car, letting conversation unfold without eye contact
- Asking open-ended questions and then listening without rushing to fix anything
- Sharing a meal without an agenda, just being together
- Respecting their privacy while still showing up consistently

One father I worked with took his daughters horseback riding every Saturday. On those rides, he was playful and open, and they talked freely. At home, he shifted into "dad mode," enforcing rules and structure. What he didn't realize was that his daughters didn't experience those as two separate roles. To them, he was always dad. The openness they felt on horseback wasn't about friendship, it was about access. And when that access felt conditional, they learned to keep their vulnerability separate from the parts of him they couldn't reliably reach.

This is the paradox of connection with teens. They may not always seek us out, but they are always watching how we show up. They notice whether we respect their growing autonomy. They notice whether we listen without judgment. They notice whether we trust them enough to let them try, while still being there if they stumble. Their signals may be subtle, but they are constant.

When we stay steady, calm, curious, and present, we give them the safety net they need to risk independence. And when we model vulnerability ourselves, saying things like "I am feeling worried, but I trust you to figure this out," we show them that connection is not about control. It is about presence.

EMOTIONAL CONTAGION

Connection is not only built through words or play. It is also built through what psychologists call **"emotional contagion."**

Have you ever been around someone brimming with joy, and you couldn't help but feel lighter? Or spent time with someone heavy with sadness, and felt yourself sink? That is emotional contagion. Our mirror neurons are designed to pick up the emotions of those around us and reflect them back. It is one of the most powerful forms of social influence we carry, often without realizing it.

Children are especially sensitive to this. They don't just hear our words, they absorb our state. If we are anxious, they feel it. If we are calm, they feel that too. This is why our presence matters more than our performance. Our emotional state is a signal, and our children read it instantly.

I saw this play out in my own life long before I became a parent. I grew up in the traditional American high school culture of the '80s and '90s, where athletes often sat at the top of the social ladder and "nerds" were pushed to the margins. By all accounts, I should have been on the outside. I was known for choir, drama, English, and math. But I carried myself with openness and curiosity. I didn't let labels define me. Instead, I approached people with genuine interest in who they were, not what group they belonged to.

That emotional stance became contagious. I found myself moving between cliques with ease, building friendships across invisible barriers. Over time, I even influenced my friends to connect with one another, to cross those same boundaries. What began as my personal mindset rippled outward into a culture of belonging. That is the power of emotional contagion. It can dismantle walls and create bridges.

As parents, this is the influence we carry every day. When we show up with empathy, curiosity, and calm, our children catch it. When we show up with fear, anger, or dismissal, they catch that too. Emotional contagion is about awareness. It is about asking ourselves: What am I transmitting right now? What atmosphere am I creating in this room?

When we model emotional regulation, when we name our feelings honestly, when we choose curiosity over judgment, we are not just teaching skills. We are shaping the emotional climate our children will carry into their friendships and classrooms, and eventually into their workplaces and families.

Emotional contagion is the invisible current of connection. It is how we teach our children to see others as individuals, to bypass stereotypes, and to create belonging wherever they go. And it begins with us.

PRACTICAL WAYS TO HARNESS EMOTIONAL CONTAGION AT HOME

Here are a few simple, everyday practices that can help you model emotional contagion intentionally:

- **Model calm in conflict:** When tensions rise, take a visible breath before responding. Children catch your pause as much as your words.
- **Name your own emotions:** Say, "I'm feeling frustrated, so I'm going to take a moment," instead of letting frustration leak out unspoken.
- **Show joy in small things:** Celebrate little wins, laugh at yourself, and let your child see delight as contagious too.
- **Practice repair out loud:** If you snap, circle back with, "That was my stress, not your fault." This teaches accountability and emotional ownership.
- **Invite curiosity:** Ask, "What are you feeling right now?" and listen without rushing to fix. This shows that emotions are safe to share.

PRACTICAL SWAPS FOR SCREEN TIME

If you find yourself relying on screens to keep your child occupied, here are three small swaps you can try today. Each one strengthens connection by restoring the unspoken signals that screens tend to interrupt.

Diaper changes: Instead of handing over a phone, sing a silly song or make exaggerated faces. This builds eye contact and emotional mirroring, two of the earliest signals of connection.

Meals: Replace screen time with a simple ritual, like sharing one "high" and one "low" from the day. This creates conversation, belonging, and the signal that "your experiences matter to me."

Car rides: Swap the tablet for storytelling. Tell a story from your childhood, or make up a silly story together. This sparks imagination and connection, and it sends the signal that being together is enough.

These swaps are not about perfection. They are about presence. Even small changes can shift the message from "the screen matters most" to "you matter most."

SIGNALS FOR REFLECTION

These questions help you notice the signals you send and receive in your relationship with your child. These reflections are not meant to judge you. They are meant to help you see the invisible communication that shapes your relationships every day.

- What are some ways you most enjoy making connections with other people?
- What do you notice about your child's ways of connecting with you and others?
- What signals has your child been sending when they are trying to connect with you?
- What signals do you send back in those moments?
- Where can you create more opportunities for connection in your daily routine?
- How can you encourage your child to build connections outside of digital formats?
- When my child looks at me, do they see my eyes or me looking at a device?

CLOSING THOUGHTS

Connection is not built from grand gestures. It is built in the daily signals we send: putting the phone down and making eye contact, the willingness to play, the calm breath when our child is upset. It is built in the way we show up, again and again, with presence.

When we prioritize connection, we are not only meeting our child's first survival instinct. We are giving them the foundation for every other aspect of their growth. Connection is the soil in which autonomy, integrity, and resilience can take root. And when we nurture it, we are not just raising children who survive. We are raising children who thrive.

THE SIGNALS OF GROWING INDEPENDENCE

The Second C: Control

HELPING CHILDREN BUILD EMOTIONAL OWNERSHIP AND INNER SAFETY

One of the most fundamental psychological needs a person has is the need for autonomy. According to the Self Determination Theory, autonomy is not about independence or isolation. Rather, it is about the feeling of agency, the sense that your actions are self-directed and aligned with your own identity. It is the experience of "I have a say in my world. I can choose. I can act. I can feel what I feel, and that feeling belongs to me."

Autonomy is a child's way of building internal control. It is not control over others, but over their own body, choices, and emotional landscape. This is how they begin to trust themselves. When that need is supported, children develop resilience, motivation, and a grounded sense of self. When it is thwarted, when they are constantly overridden, coerced, or dismissed, they may comply on the outside but feel disconnected on the inside.

This chapter is about that need. It is about how autonomy begins in the body, how it shows up in everyday moments, and how we can support it without slipping into control. It is about helping children build emotional ownership, not by giving them free rein, but by offering real choices, honoring their signals, and modeling what it looks like to trust yourself.

THE FIRST LANGUAGE OF AUTONOMY

Long before children have the words to express their needs, they express them through their bodies. A baby arches away from a spoon. A toddler flings off a jacket. A preschooler refuses to hold your hand in the parking lot. These are not random acts. They are early expressions of agency.

The body is the first place where autonomy lives. It is where children begin to say, "I know something about myself, even if I cannot explain it yet." And often, that knowing shows up as resistance.

I remember when Connor was two and refused to wear socks. It was winter. I was frustrated. I tried reasoning, bribing, even sneaking them on while he was distracted. Nothing worked. Eventually, I sat down and asked, "What is wrong with the socks?" He said, "They squeeze." That was it. The size was too small and they hurt him. Once I found a larger pair, he wore them happily.

It was not about the socks. It was about sensation. It was about control. It was about being listened to.

Autonomy often begins with sensation. A child's body is usually their first boundary, and honoring it teaches them that their inner signals matter. Their discomfort is not a problem to fix. It is a message to understand.

This is especially true in moments that feel inconvenient. A toddler refuses a hug from a relative. A preschooler insists on wearing shorts in the rain. A child says, "Stop tickling me," even though they were laughing a moment ago. These are not power struggles. They are boundary setting practices, real expressions of self that help children learn how to claim their voice and test their autonomy.

When we override these signals because we are in a rush, feel embarrassed, or think we know better, we unintentionally teach children to override themselves. We teach them that their body is negotiable. That their "no" is conditional.

But when we pause, when we listen, when we say, "OK, let us figure this out together," we do something else entirely. We teach them that their body is trustworthy. That their instincts are worth honoring. That they are allowed to feel what they feel and choose what they choose, even when it is messy.

This is the first language of autonomy. It is not polished or verbal. It is raw, sensory, and often inconvenient. But it is sacred. And when we learn to read it, we become the kind of adults who raise children who trust themselves.

REAL CHOICE AND FALSE CHOICE

Children are exquisitely attuned to power dynamics. They know when a choice is real and when it is performative. "Do you want the red cup or the blue cup" is a real choice. "Do you want to clean up now or lose your screen time" is not.

When we offer choices that preserve dignity and agency, we build trust. When we disguise control as choice, we erode it.

Children may comply, but they learn to distrust the invitation. They learn that "choice" is often code for "do what I say."

One friend shared a story with me that still sits heavy in my chest. Her daughter had been struggling with transitions, getting dressed, leaving the house, shifting from play to cleanup. She was trying to be gentle and offer options. But one day, she said, "You can choose to get dressed now or lose your playdate later." Her daughter froze. Then she whispered with tears in her eyes, "That is not a real choice, mommy." And she was right.

My friend cried telling me that story. Not because she had done something terrible, but because she had seen it clearly. She had meant well. She was trying to avoid yelling, trying to stay calm. But in that moment, she realized she had wrapped control in the language of autonomy. And her daughter had seen through it.

That is the thing about children. They may not have the vocabulary, but they have the wisdom. They know when their voice matters and when it is being managed. They know when a choice is safe and when it is loaded.

And when they do not see through it, when they accept disguised control as truth, they often internalize a quieter message, "My choices do not really count." Over time, they may stop reaching for autonomy altogether. They might become overly compliant, overly cautious, or overly attuned to what others want. This does not mean they lack agency. It means they have learned that agency is not welcome.

This does not always show up as rebellion. Sometimes it shows up as perfectionism. As people pleasing. As a child who asks, "Is this OK?" before making every decision. When real choice is missing, children may begin to outsource their instincts. They look to us not just for guidance, but for permission to exist.

That is why honest choice matters. Not just for behavior, but for identity. When we offer choices that are real, we help children build a sense of self that is sturdy, not performative. We teach them that their voice is not just tolerated. It is trusted.

When we move beyond performative options and offer choices that are truly meaningful, we reinforce that trust. It is not about giving children endless decisions. It is about offering ones that matter.

"You can choose whether to eat now or later." "You can decide if you want help or want to try it on your own."

These choices say, "I trust you to listen to yourself." They also say, "I am not afraid of your process. I am not here to steer you toward the outcome I prefer. I am here to support you in learning how to choose."

This does not mean we avoid boundaries. It means we are honest about them. "It will be time to leave in five minutes. You can choose what shoes to wear." That is a boundary with autonomy inside it. "You can choose to cooperate or lose privileges" is a threat dressed as a choice.

When we offer real choices, we teach children that their voice matters. That their instincts are worth listening to. That their needs are not being managed, but met.

And when we mess it up, and we will, we can name it. We can say, "That was not a real choice. I was trying to control the outcome. I am sorry." That repair is powerful. It teaches children that even grown-ups are still learning how to honor autonomy.

AUTONOMY IS NOT REBELLION

It is easy to mistake autonomy for rebellion. A child says "no," and we feel rejected. A teenager pulls away, and we feel abandoned. But autonomy is not rejection. It is expansion.

When a child asserts themselves, they are not pushing us away. They are pulling themselves forward. They are practicing the art of being a person. And that practice requires space.

I once coached a parent whose daughter refused to wear the outfit laid out for her on picture day. The mother was heartbroken, because she had chosen it with love. But the daughter wanted to wear a mismatched ensemble with sparkly boots and a superhero cape. "She ruined the photo," the mother said. But when we reframed it, she saw something else. Her daughter was not rejecting her, she was claiming herself.

I have lived this lesson too. Connor and I have had our share of what I call "the outerwear wars." On a cold morning, I would insist on a jacket, and he would insist he did not need one. At first, I saw it as stubbornness. But over time, I realized it was something else: his body runs warmer than mine, and he was learning to trust his own senses about it. I also had to remember that children do not yet have the pattern recognition that we as adults take for granted. They have not had years of experience contrasting the feeling of being cozy inside a warm house to the shock of stepping out into cold winter air. To them, the warmth of the living room is their reality, and they cannot yet anticipate how different it will feel outside.

So instead of forcing the coat, I invited him to step outside and feel the air for himself. Sometimes he still refused, and I would simply say, "It is your body, it is your choice. I will bring your coat in case you change your mind." More often than not, by the time we reached school, he would ask for it. And when he did, I handed it over without a single "I told you so."

That moment was not about winning or losing. It was about giving him space to practice autonomy safely, to learn from his own experience, and to know that changing his mind was not failure, but wisdom.

Autonomy is the emotional version of learning to walk. It is the child saying, "I am learning to hold my own feelings, my own choices, my own voice."

WHEN AUTONOMY TRIGGERS US

It is hard when a child says "no." It is hard when they reject our help, our advice, our comfort. It can feel personal. But autonomy is not rejection. It is practice. Each "no" is a child practicing the art of being separate, of holding their own ground, of testing whether their voice has weight in the world.

When we feel triggered, we can pause and ask ourselves, "What is this touching in me?" Often, it is not just about the child in front of us. It is about our own history with control. Maybe we grew up in a home where "no" was dangerous, where resistance was punished, or where compliance was the only way to stay safe. Maybe we carry a fear of chaos, or a longing to be needed, and our child's independence brushes against those tender places.

My father once told me that my mother was a wonderful mother until we girls started saying "no." That was when she struggled. She did not know how to meet our resistance without yelling, inventing new chores, or threatening punishment. To her, our "no" felt like defiance. To us, it was simply the first fragile expression of independence. That memory often surfaces when Connor says "no." It reminds me that my reaction is not only about him. It is also about the echoes of my own childhood.

When Connor was five, he refused to eat dinner. I felt the

urge to control, to insist, to threaten taking away dessert. But instead, I said, "You do not have to eat, but your body will probably feel hungry later. You can decide." He did not eat. Later, he asked for a snack. I reminded him that dinner was still available, and he chose to eat it. That moment was not really about food. It was about control. He needed to feel that the decision was his.

Parents often worry that nutrition is nonnegotiable, and they are right. Within this framework, the parent's role is to provide healthy food consistently, to set the rhythm of mealtimes, and to model balanced eating. The child's role is to decide whether and how much to eat. When parents focus on offering rather than forcing, they avoid turning meals into battles. Over time, children learn to trust both their hunger cues and the steady presence of nourishing food.

Children push back not because they want to reject us, but because they are learning to trust themselves. They are experimenting with ownership. They are asking, "Am I allowed to be me, even when it is inconvenient for you?"

When we respond with curiosity instead of control, we create space for growth, both theirs and ours. We show them that their "no" is not dangerous, and that our love is not conditionally based on their compliance. And we show ourselves that letting go of control does not mean losing connection. In fact, it often deepens it.

TEACHING EMOTIONAL OWNERSHIP

Autonomy is not just about choices. It is about feelings. Emotional ownership is not something children are born with. It is something they learn through modeling, language, and repair.

Children do not yet have the neurological maturity to separate having a feeling from being consumed by a feeling. Their prefrontal cortex, the part of the brain that helps regulate and reflect, is still under construction. So when a child is angry, sad, or ashamed, it can feel like a totality that consumes them. They are not thinking, "I am experiencing anger." They are thinking, "I am anger." That is why our modeling matters so much.

When we say, "You are feeling angry, and that is OK. Let's find a way to move through it," we teach them that emotions are signals, not threats. When we say, "You are making me angry," we unintentionally teach them to outsource responsibility for emotions that are ours to own.

I remember a moment when Connor was having a meltdown over a broken toy. My initial reaction was to say, "It is OK, it is just a toy." But I caught myself. I knelt down and said, "You are really sad about this, huh" He nodded through tears. "It was one of my favorites." That moment of naming gave him permission to feel. And once he felt seen, the storm passed.

Another time, when Connor was in first grade, he hid his homework for weeks in a cubby at the aftercare program. When the truth finally came out, he sobbed with shame. My first impulse was anger, he had lied, and I felt betrayed. But then I realized this was a moment to teach emotional ownership. He already felt the weight of his mistake. What he needed was not more shame, but a model of how to hold it. So I said, "I can see how heavy this feels for you. You made a choice you regret, and now you are telling the truth. That is brave. Let us figure out how to move forward." That moment taught him that mistakes do not erase worth, and that emotions, even hard ones like guilt, can be carried with honesty instead of hidden in fear.

When we name emotions without judgment, we help children build emotional literacy. When we validate emotions without rescuing, we help them build emotional resilience. And when we model our own emotional ownership, saying things like, "I am feeling overwhelmed, so I am going to take a breath," or "I snapped at you earlier, and that was not fair. That was my frustration, not your fault," we show them that feelings are not problems to solve. They are signals to honor.

This is the heart of emotional ownership: teaching children that their feelings belong to them, that they are safe to feel, and that they can move through emotions without being defined by them. And just as importantly, showing them that adults are still practicing too.

THE LONG ARC OF AUTONOMY

Autonomy does not arrive all at once. It unfolds. It stretches. It stumbles. The toddler who says "no" becomes the teen who says, "I've got this."

I often describe the invisible thread between parent and child as the "psychic umbilical cord." Just as the physical cord nourishes a baby in the womb, this unseen cord nourishes a child's sense of safety in the world. It is the felt connection that says, "I am tethered to you, even when I am separate from you."

In the early years, the cord feels short and strong. A baby cries and we respond. A toddler wanders a few feet away, then runs back for reassurance. As children grow, the cord does not disappear, it loosens. It stretches across classrooms, sleepovers, and eventually across continents. What matters is not that we cut it, but that we trust it.

Our job is not to sever the cord. Our job is to let it stretch with love. To know that connection does not require control, it requires presence. When children feel that the cord is intact, they can risk more, explore more, and return when they need grounding.

This is why autonomy is not a phase to survive. It is a relationship to nurture. Each "no" is not a rejection of us, but a tug on the cord, testing its strength. Each step toward independence is not a severing, but a stretching. And when we allow that stretch, we teach our children the most important truth of all, "You are free to grow, and you are never alone."

SIGNALS FOR REFLECTION

- What signals does my child send when they are trying to assert independence?
- How do I typically respond to those signals: with curiosity, control, or something else?
- When my child says "no," what feelings come up in me, and where do those feelings come from?
- Am I offering real choices, or am I offering choices that steer my child toward the outcome I prefer?
- What signals does my child send when they feel overwhelmed by too much autonomy?
- How do I model emotional ownership in my own life?
- Where might I be overriding my child's bodily cues or instincts without realizing it?
- What would it look like to trust my child's process a little more this week?

Autonomy is not a milestone. It is a relationship. It is the ongoing dance between connection and independence, between guidance and trust.

When we honor a child's autonomy, we are not letting go of them. We are letting go of the illusion that we must shape every part of them. We are saying, "I trust your process. I trust your voice. I trust your becoming."

Autonomy grows best in the presence of a steady, grounded adult who can hold space for a child's unfolding without rushing it, shaping it, or fearing it. Children do not need us to be perfect. They need us to be present. They need us to stay connected even when they pull away, and to stay steady even when they push back.

And as children grow, their autonomy does not float freely. It lives within the natural limits of life. These limits, the ones that shape how we move through the world, are what I call the Four Boundaries of Living. Understanding these boundaries helps us see autonomy not as something separate, but as something that grows inside a larger structure. In the next chapter, we will explore these boundaries more fully and look at how they guide children toward a deeper sense of safety, responsibility, and belonging.

CHAPTER 8

THE FOUR BOUNDARIES OF LIVING

How Children Learn to Move Within Life's Limits

THE EDGES THAT HELP CHILDREN GROW

As children grow, they do not just learn who they are, they learn *where* they are. Boundaries give shape to that learning. They help children understand the limits of their bodies, their relationships, their communities, and their choices. When we teach boundaries with clarity and compassion, we give children the structure that makes autonomy feel safe.

Autonomy does not exist in isolation. It grows within the natural limits of life itself. Children are constantly learning how to navigate the boundaries of mortality, society, relationships, and self. These boundaries shape their choices, their safety, and their sense of belonging. When we understand these boundaries, we can better recognize the signals children send as they bump up against limits that feel confusing, overwhelming, or new.

THE FRAMEWORK OF THE FOUR BOUNDARIES

One of the most profound insights I have gained through intimate experiences of death and dying, is what I call the Four Boundaries of Living. These boundaries shape the contours of our existence, and when we teach our children how to recognize and navigate them, we equip them with the tools to move through life with greater resilience, adaptability, and emotional maturity. It is important to note that how these boundaries look will vary across culture and family circumstances.

Rather than beginning with the most intimate boundary, as I often do with clients, let us start from the outermost edge and move inward.

1. THE BOUNDARY OF MORTALITY

The foremost absolute boundary is death. The bodies we inhabit are impermanent. No matter how much we optimize our health or extend our vitality, we are all subject to the finite nature of life. As my mother used to say, "Ah, life...no one ever gets out of it alive."

This boundary teaches us humility. It reminds us that we are part of nature, not above it. We cannot leap from a plane without a parachute and expect to defy gravity. We cannot live as though we are the exception to life's rules. And yet, many of us do, until we are forced to reckon with the limits of our physical form.

When a family pet dies, a child often asks where the pet went or why it could not stay. This is an early encounter with the boundary of mortality. Being honest with them at this highly emotional moment serves not to frighten them, but to help them understand that life has a beginning and an end.

When children understand that life has a natural endpoint,

they begin to appreciate the value of time, the importance of safety, and the sacredness of being alive.

2. THE BOUNDARY OF SOCIETY

Humans are social, communal creatures. We evolved through cooperation, mutual reliance, and shared responsibility. Our brains are wired to seek connection, and our survival has always depended on our ability to live within communities.

Societal boundaries are the rules and norms that allow us to coexist. They are not fixed, they can and should evolve, but they must also be respected and negotiated collectively. When we teach children that rules exist to protect the whole, not just the individual, we help them develop empathy and civic responsibility.

This does not mean suppressing individuality. In fact, advocating for one's needs within a societal framework is essential. But it must be done with clarity, compassion, and a willingness to help others understand, not to argue or dominate. As I often say to my clients, "Advocate, do not agitate."

A child who starts to run across the street without looking is not being reckless, they simply have not yet learned the societal boundary of shared safety. Guiding them to pause, look, and wait helps them understand that some rules exist to protect everyone, not just themselves.

Children send many signals as they learn these boundaries, sometimes through resistance, sometimes through confusion, and sometimes through attempts to test whether the rules are steady or negotiable. These signals are invitations for us to teach, not to overpower.

3. THE BOUNDARY OF RELATIONSHIPS

Interpersonal boundaries govern the space between ourselves and others. These include relationships with family, friends, colleagues, and intimate partners. Unlike societal boundaries, which are often systemized, interpersonal boundaries are fluid. They shift with time, context, and personal growth.

Healthy relationships require communication, flexibility, and mutual respect. If your child is struggling with a friend or sibling, it is an opportunity to teach them how to express their needs, listen actively, and negotiate expectations. For example, if one child prefers quiet time after school, it is important they communicate that choice clearly and respectfully. The boundary is crossed when they begin insisting that others stop playing or reading nearby, rather than finding a compromise. Respecting relationships means honoring your own needs without coercing or forcing others to follow them.

When siblings argue over a toy, each child is learning the relational boundary of "my space, your space." Helping them express their needs without overpowering each other teaches them how to navigate relationships with respect.

Children who learn to navigate interpersonal boundaries become adults who can sustain meaningful relationships without losing themselves or overpowering others.

4. THE BOUNDARY OF SELF

At the core lies our personal boundaries, the space of autonomy, agency, and self-determination. According to Deci and Ryan's Self Determination Theory, autonomy is one of the three fundamental human needs. It is the ability to make choices that reflect one's values, desires, and sense of self.

Personal boundaries often affect no one but ourselves, yet

they ripple outward. Take time management, for instance. If your child is chronically late, they may miss out on opportunities, strain relationships, or face consequences that ultimately impact their well-being.

A child who says, "I need a break," or "I do not like loud noises," is practicing the boundary of self. They are learning to recognize their internal limits and communicate them clearly, a skill many adults are still learning.

Children send clear signals when they are nearing the edge of their internal boundaries, through withdrawal, irritability, sensory overwhelm, or sudden refusal. When we respond with steadiness rather than pressure, we help them learn to trust those signals, instead of overriding them.

Teaching children to honor their own boundaries while recognizing how boundaries shape their actions and the impact their actions have on others, is a cornerstone of emotional intelligence. It is where autonomy meets accountability.

HOW BOUNDARIES SHAPE AUTONOMY

When we guide our children through the Four Boundaries of Living, we are not just teaching them how to behave. We are teaching them how to belong, how to thrive, and how to honor both themselves and the world around them.

Ultimately, lasting satisfaction with who we are and how we choose to show up in the world begins with feeling at peace with the choices we make for our own bodies. That is the truest expression of autonomy.

- What signals does my child send when they are approaching a boundary? Are they emotional, relational, societal, and/or physical?
- How do I typically respond when my child bumps up against a limit: with clarity, frustration, softness, or inconsistency?
- Which boundaries in our home feel clear and steady, and which ones feel confusing or negotiable?
- What signals do I send when I set a boundary: calm leadership, uncertainty, or something else?
- How do I model to my child what it looks like to live within my own boundaries around time, energy, commitments and relationships?
- Where might my child need more structure to feel safe, and where might they need more space to practice autonomy?
- How do cultural, family, or personal values shape the boundaries I set?
- What would it look like to hold boundaries with clarity and compassion, without slipping into control or rigidity?

CLOSING THOUGHTS

Boundaries are not walls. They are the edges that help children understand themselves and the world. When children learn to navigate all four boundaries, they do not just grow into independence, they grow into wholeness.

Boundaries give autonomy shape. Autonomy gives boundaries meaning.

Together, they help children become grounded, capable, emotionally secure humans.

And when we teach boundaries with steadiness and compassion, we are not limiting our children. We are giving them a map. We are helping them understand where they can move freely and where life asks them to pause, listen, or adjust. These boundaries are not punishments or constraints. They are the natural contours of being human, the quiet structure that allows freedom to feel safe.

Children learn these boundaries slowly, through trial and error, through the signals their bodies send, through the feedback they receive from relationships, and through the rhythms of the world around them. They learn by testing, by stretching, by bumping up against limits that feel confusing or frustrating. And each time they do, they are not misbehaving. They are learning how to live.

Our role is not to shield them from these boundaries or to enforce them with rigidity. Our role is to guide them with clarity, to hold the edges with warmth, and to stay present as they discover what each boundary means for them. When we do this, we help them build a sense of safety that comes from the inside, not from fear or compliance.

Children who understand boundaries learn how to care for their bodies, how to move through communities with respect, how to build relationships that honor both themselves and others, and how to listen to the quiet signals of their own inner world. They learn that freedom is not the absence of limits, but the ability to move confidently within them.

And perhaps most importantly, they learn that boundaries are not something done to them. Boundaries are something they can participate in, shape, and eventually hold for themselves.

When we teach boundaries this way, we are not just preparing children for childhood. We are preparing them for life. We are giving them the tools to navigate loss, responsibility, intimacy, and self-respect. We are helping them grow into adults who can honor their own limits without shame and honor the limits of others without fear.

This is the deeper promise of boundaries. They do not restrict a child's becoming. They protect it, and give it room to unfold with integrity, clarity, and connection.

THE POWER OF ACCOMPLISHMENT

The Third C: Competency

FROM AUTONOMY TO COMPETENCY

Having explored how autonomy takes root within the Four Boundaries of Living, we now turn to the next question: How do children carry that sense of agency into the wider world of responsibility, relationships, and growth? The answer lies in the third core need of the Self Determination Theory: competency.

Competency is the **scaffolding of mastery**. Just as scaffolding supports a building while it rises, children need temporary structures of guidance, feedback, practice, and play that allow them to climb higher than they could alone. And just like scaffolding, our support is not meant to stay forever. It is meant to be gradually removed as their confidence and skills strengthen.

WHAT COMPETENCY REALLY MEANS

Competency is not about perfection. It is not about being the best. It is about the lived experience of an inner knowing: *I can do this. I can try. I can learn.*

Psychologists define competency as "the experience of mastery and being effective in one's activity." In practice, it is much more than that. Competency is the bridge between effort and identity. It is the moment when a child moves from "I don't know if I can" to "I know I can try."

Children develop competency when three conditions are present:

- **Optimal challenge:** The task is hard enough to stretch them, but not so hard that it overwhelms them.
- **Opportunity to initiate:** They are given the chance to try, even if it means fumbling or failing.
- **Meaningful feedback:** They receive guidance that encourages growth, not shame.

When these three pillars are in place, children begin to internalize a powerful truth: *I am capable of learning, and my effort matters.* And along the way, they send signals through hesitation, excitement, frustration, or persistence, which show us exactly where they are in the learning process.

Many children carry distorted beliefs about what it means to be competent. They may think: *I have to be good at everything.* Or: *If I fail once, it means I am not capable.* These beliefs are corrosive. They turn learning into comparison and effort into shame. Part of our role as parents is to dismantle these myths by modeling a healthier truth: No one is good at everything, mistakes are part of growth, and effort is more important than outcome.

Competency also evolves across development. In early childhood, it looks like tying shoes or pouring cereal. In middle childhood, it expands into academics, sports, and friendships. In adolescence, it becomes tied to identity. Teens want to know not just *what can I do* but *who am I becoming.*

I remember as a child thinking my mom was the smartest person alive. She could spell any word, solve any math problem, and insisted that I learn to drive a stick shift because she knew how, even though she did not drive one herself. Years later, when Connor said, "Mommy, you just know everything, don't you?" I answered honestly: "I appreciate you thinking that, but no, Connor, I definitely don't. I just know where to go to find answers, and I can teach you that too."

That moment mattered. Because competency is not about intelligence. It is about resourcefulness. It is about knowing that you do not have to have all the answers, but you can learn how to find them. That is the scaffolding that will hold him long after I am gone.

THE FIRST STEPS: SELF-HELP AND ADAPTIVE SKILLS

Competency begins in the smallest of moments:

- A toddler tying their own shoes.
- A preschooler brushing their teeth.
- A child pouring their own cereal, even if milk spills across the counter.

These are not inconveniences. They are scaffolding moments that allow children to practice mastery. When we step in too quickly, we unintentionally send the message: "I don't believe you can do this." And children send signals right back through pride when they succeed, frustration when they struggle, or resistance when they feel over-helped.

I remember when Connor was three and insisted on buckling his own car seat. We were running late, and my instinct was to lean over and snap it in place. But I stopped myself. His little fingers fumbled, the strap twisted, and it took twice as long as it would have if I had done it. But when he finally clicked it into place, the look on his face was pure pride. That moment was not about efficiency. It was about ownership.

These early self-help skills are the foundation of competency. They are the first rungs of the scaffolding. Each time a child is allowed to try, even imperfectly, they are building the belief: *I am capable. My effort matters.*

THE VALUE OF DISCERNMENT

Not every skill is essential. Competency is not about doing everything. It is about knowing which skills matter most for the individual. This is where **discernment** comes in.

In our home, video games represent a great example. Connor and his father both enjoy playing them, and I can see the value they bring: problem-solving, teamwork, creativity, and even stress relief. I play sometimes too, but not nearly as much as they do. When we are all relaxing after school and work, I often choose to read or listen to a book, do a puzzle, or play a painting game on my phone instead.

When Connor asks why, I tell him honestly: "I know video games can be fun, but I also really enjoy reading and creative games. They help me feel calm and grounded; they help me relax." That conversation shows him that competency is not about doing everything. It is about choosing wisely where to place your energy.

Discernment is the scaffolding that helps children prioritize. It teaches them that they do not need to climb every ladder, only the ones that matter most to them. And it also teaches them that what matters can look different for each person. For one child, video games may be a meaningful way to connect with friends. For another, it may be art, sports, or music. The skill is not in doing it all, but in learning how to choose. And children often send signals about what nourishes them and what drains them, long before they have the words to explain it.

THE POWER OF PLAY

Play is the natural scaffolding of childhood. It is how children practice life before the stakes feel high. In play, they experiment, negotiate, and discover. They learn to take risks without fear of failure. They learn that effort matters more than outcome.

When I washed dishes with Connor as a preschooler, water splashed everywhere. Towels lay soaked on the counters and floor. But the lesson was not about clean dishes. It was about joy, effort, and the pride of "I did it myself." That messy kitchen was scaffolding. It gave him a safe place to practice mastery while still feeling connected to me.

Play is not frivolous. Neuroscience shows that during play, the brain is flooded with dopamine and other neurochemicals that strengthen learning and memory. Play literally wires the brain for curiosity, problem-solving, and resilience. It is the most natural way children learn because it keeps motivation intrinsic.

There are many forms of play, with each scaffolding type teaching different skills:

- Solitary play builds focus and imagination.
- Parallel play (two children playing side by side) builds comfort with social presence.
- Cooperative play teaches negotiation, compromise, and empathy.
- Imaginative play allows children to try on roles, test boundaries, and explore identity.

I have seen this unfold on playgrounds. A child climbs the ladder to the slide, hesitates at the top, and then finally lets go. The cheers from friends are not about speed or grace. They are about courage. That moment is not just fun. It is practice for every future leap that the child will take in life.

With Connor, I notice that play often reveals his natural problem-solving instincts. When he builds elaborate Lego structures or invents rules for a new game, he is not just entertaining himself. He is practicing leadership, creativity, and persistence. He is learning that he can create something from nothing. These moments are signals too, glimpses into what lights him up, what challenges him, and what helps him grow.

Play says: "I don't know this perfectly, but I can try." And that is the heart of competency. It is scaffolding disguised as joy.

OWNING OUR MISTAKES

Competency is not built by avoiding mistakes. It is built by owning them.

A friend once told me: "A mistake is just a missed take." That reframing matters. Mistakes are not evidence of failure. They are scaffolding. They are the temporary structures that help us climb higher.

Children watch us closely. When they see us apologize,

repair, and try again, they learn that mistakes are not the end of the story, they are part of the process. If, instead, they see us cover up, deflect, or berate ourselves, they absorb that too. Our response to our own mistakes becomes the blueprint for their inner voice.

A parent promises a child they will go to the park after errands. The day runs long, and the parent doesn't follow through. The child is disappointed. Instead of brushing it off, the parent says, "I broke my promise, and I know that hurt. I'll make sure we go tomorrow." The child sees that accountability matters more than perfection, and that trust can be rebuilt through honesty and repair.

A child spills juice across the carpet, and the parent snaps in frustration: "Why weren't you more careful?" The child's face falls, shoulders curling inward. Later, the parent kneels beside them and says, "I was wrong to yell. Spills happen. I should have helped you clean it up calmly." Together, they wipe the stain, side by side. The repair matters more than the carpet. The child learns that mistakes are not catastrophes—they are invitations to practice patience and forgiveness.

Owning mistakes also teaches empathy. When children see us admit we were wrong, they learn that everyone is fallible, and that relationships can survive imperfection. It softens their expectations of themselves and others.

I think of the times I have burned dinner, was late for a meeting, or forgot a commitment. When I name those mistakes out loud, without spiraling into shame, I am teaching Connor that mistakes are not catastrophes. They are information. They are invitations to adjust. And often, the way a child reacts to a mistake, shrinking, melting down, laughing it off, or trying again, is a signal of how safe they feel in the learning process.

This is the deeper truth: Mistakes are not cracks in the foundation. They are scaffolding. They hold us steady while we learn, and then they fall away once the lesson is integrated.

And sometimes what looks like a mistake, or what gets mislabeled as "immaturity," is really another signal that additional or ongoing scaffolding is needed.

IMMATURITY OR A SIGNAL FOR SCAFFOLDING?

During a parent-teacher conference once, Connor's teacher described him as "a little immature." At first, the word seemed harmless, but it risked dismissing something more complex.

Connor does not usually struggle to sit still. What he does struggle with is holding back words that come rushing out. He blurts things in the middle of lessons, sometimes playful noises like "arrr arr," and often tries to talk to his friends when the class is meant to be quiet. These are not signs of immaturity. They are signals of a mind that has trouble pressing pause, a brain that struggles with inhibition and timing.

Experts on ADHD (Attention-Deficit/Hyperactivity Disorder) remind us that these behaviors are not laziness or defiance. They are expressions of executive function challenges. To call them "immaturity" is to miss the deeper truth that Connor's behaviors are not a phase to outgrow but a language to be understood.

When we label a child as "immature," we risk overlooking the scaffolding they need. Scaffolding is the structure that helps a child practice skills they do not yet have—the gentle supports that allow them to grow into regulation, connection, and confidence.

The invitation, then, is to pause before we label. To ask ourselves: *What is this behavior trying to tell me? What support might help this child practice what they cannot yet manage on their own?* Because when we shift from judgment to curiosity, we stop seeing a child who is "behind" and start seeing a child who is asking for help in the only way they can.

Just as blurting or disruptive behavior can be reframed as a call for scaffolding, so too can boredom—often misunderstood as a problem—become one of the most powerful supports for growth.

THE GIFT OF BOREDOM

Competency also grows in the quiet spaces, those unscheduled, unstructured hours when children must invent their own fun.

Boredom is often misunderstood. Adults tend to see it as a problem to be solved, a gap to be filled. Yet boredom can be a gift. It is the scaffolding that supports imagination, innovation, and resilience. When children are bored, their brains are not idle. Neuroscience shows that the "default mode network" of the brain becomes active, the same network linked to creativity, problem-solving, and self-reflection. In other words, boredom is the soil where new ideas take root.

Boredom also teaches emotional regulation. Sitting with the discomfort of "nothing to do" builds frustration tolerance. It teaches children that they can move through restlessness without panicking, that they can generate their own solutions rather than waiting for someone else to entertain them.

I remember long summer afternoons and weekends as a child when my siblings and I were told to "go outside and play with your friends." Many other friends and kids of our generation were told, "Don't come back until the streetlights turn on." We built forts, took hikes through the woods, and invented elaborate games while arguing fiercely about the rules. Those hours were not wasted. They were training grounds for creativity, negotiation, and resilience.

With Connor, I notice that when he is bored, he often gets

creative with scissors and tape, "fixing" things around the house. He will patch up a balloon, repair a toy, or reinforce his swords and shields. Boredom is not empty time. It is an invitation to invent, to tinker, to make something new out of what is already there. That kind of play is not just entertainment. It is practice in problem-solving, persistence, and resourcefulness. These moments are signals too, signs of where a child's curiosity naturally pulls them when the world gets quiet.

And boredom is not just a gift for children. As an adult, I have noticed that some of my best ideas come when I allow myself to be still. When I put down my phone, resist the urge to fill every gap with productivity, and simply sit with my thoughts, creativity begins to surface. Some of my strongest writing insights and coaching frameworks have emerged in those quiet, "boring" moments—on a walk without headphones, in the shower, or while staring out the window. Boredom, for me, has become a teacher too. It reminds me that silence is not wasted time. It is fertile ground.

When every moment is scheduled, or distraction is provided at every turn in the form of technology, children and adults alike lose this practice. We become dependent on external stimulation and may struggle to tolerate stillness. But when we allow downtime, we give ourselves and our children the scaffolding of self-discovery. We teach that we are not passive consumers of life, but active creators of it.

A RENAISSANCE SPIRIT

Competency is not about mastering one narrow skill. It is about cultivating curiosity across many domains. I call this the **Renaissance spirit**, the freedom to explore art, science, music, storytelling, and invention.

The Renaissance was a period of extraordinary growth because people dared to cross boundaries. Artists studied anatomy to paint more realistically. Scientists wrote poetry. Inventors sketched flying machines while also designing bridges. Their genius was not in doing one thing perfectly, but in allowing curiosity to spill across disciplines. That same spirit is what children need today.

When children are encouraged to dabble, to try, to explore, they learn something profound: "I am not limited to one path. I can learn anything." This is not about raising prodigies. It is about raising children who see themselves as capable of growth in many directions.

With Connor, I see this Renaissance spirit when he moves fluidly between worlds. One afternoon he is cutting and taping together shields and swords, inventing elaborate battles. The next he is asking questions about the solar system, or sketching deeply imaginative worlds, or cracking and scrambling eggs in the kitchen. None of these pursuits may become his lifelong passion, but each one builds the belief that he can try, explore, and grow.

Psychologists call this **transfer of learning**, the ability to take skills from one domain and apply them in another. A child who experiments with rhythm in music may later use that same sense of pattern in math. A child who builds forts may later use those problem-solving skills in engineering or leadership. The Renaissance spirit is scaffolding for adaptability. It teaches children that knowledge is not compartmentalized. It is interconnected.

This attitude also protects against perfectionism. When children are allowed to try many things, they learn that it is normal to be a beginner. They discover the joy of learning for its own sake, not just for achievement. They learn that failure in one area does not define them, because there are always other ladders to climb.

The Renaissance spirit is not about scattering energy aimlessly. It is about cultivating a mindset of openness, curiosity, and resilience. It is about teaching children that they are not confined to a single identity, but are capable of becoming many things over time. And often, the activities they return to repeatedly are signals of where their natural interests and strengths may be unfolding.

This is the deepest form of competency. Not just knowing how to do something, but knowing how to learn. It is the scaffolding that prepares them to build a life of curiosity, adaptability, and wonder.

SIGNALS FOR REFLECTION

- What is something I did as a child without adult supervision that made me feel competent?
- Where did I feel most effective, most capable, most alive?
- What skills do I most want my child to carry into adulthood?
- How can I create opportunities for my child to practice, fail, and try again without rescuing them too soon?
- Am I modeling discernment in my own life, choosing where to place my energy with intention?
- Do I secretly expect my child to be good at everything, or do I allow them to specialize, stumble, and grow at their own pace?
- When my child makes a mistake, do I treat it as evidence of failure, or as scaffolding, a temporary support on the way to mastery? Am I modeling that failure as a part of growing and learning?
- Where in my parenting am I providing too much or too little

scaffolding? Where might I need to step back so my child can climb on their own? Where might I need to provide additional support?

- Do I allow boredom to be a teacher, trusting that creativity and resilience often emerge from stillness?
- Am I encouraging a renaissance spirit in my child, giving them permission to explore many paths and discover that learning itself is the skill that lasts?
- What signals does my child send when they feel capable, overwhelmed, curious, or discouraged, and how do I respond to those signals?

CLOSING THOUGHTS

Competency is not a checklist. It is a relationship with effort, failure, and growth. It is the ongoing dance between challenge and support, between trying and trying again.

When we nurture competency, we are not raising children who can do everything. We are raising children who believe: I can learn. I can try. I can grow.

That belief is what carries them forward through school, through friendships, and through the long arc of life. It is what allows them to face mistakes with resilience, boredom with creativity, and new challenges with curiosity.

Competency is the scaffolding of mastery. It is not the finished building, but the framework that makes growth possible. And when we trust our children to climb, stumble, and climb again, we give them the confidence to one day stand tall on their own, ready to keep building, exploring, and becoming.

CHAPTER 10

EMOTIONS AREN'T A SWITCH YOU CAN FLIP

Emotional Development as a Learned Skill

FROM COMPETENCY TO EMOTIONAL GROWTH

In the last chapter, we explored competency as the scaffolding of mastery. But scaffolding is not only for skills like tying shoes or solving math problems. It is also for the inner world. Just as children need support to build confidence in what they can *do*, they also need guidance to understand what they can *feel*.

This is where emotional development comes in. And here's the truth: Emotions are not automatic. They are not a switch you can flip. Emotional development is a learned skill. The signals children receive from us about how feelings work become the foundation for how they learn to navigate their own inner landscape.

RELEARNING EMOTION AS WE TEACH IT

Think of a human as a factory-built computer. We come pre-loaded with certain features: personality traits, behavioral tendencies, even survival emotions like fear, anger, and empathy. But one thing is missing: emotional processing.

Emotional development is not automatic. It is learned, just like walking, reading, or tying shoelaces. Understanding and managing emotions takes time, guidance, and practice.

Many parents assume that kids will just "know" how to feel and express themselves. But they don't. Parenting means guiding children to understand the intricate pulse of their inner world. It means teaching, cultivating, modeling, and most importantly, practicing emotional presence with them daily.

And here's the deeper reality: When we become parents, we're not just teaching our children. We're relearning for ourselves. My sister Mori once said, "No one teaches you that it's your responsibility to go back to the drawing board when you become a parent." She's right. Parenting requires us to relearn our own emotional signals while guiding our child's. That's the invisible curriculum of parenting.

I once worked with a client who was determined not to be like her "closed-off" mother. Her mother never yelled or raised her voice, but she also never laughed a full belly laugh, never rolled her eyes with playful sarcasm, and never cried in front of her children. She kept her emotions tucked behind what my client called her "proper lady" mask.

My client wanted something different. She wanted her kids to see her feelings. But she was scared. She had learned how to talk about her emotions, but showing them, actually letting them be seen, was new territory. She realized she was afraid of being too emotional in front of her kids, and worried she might do it "wrong."

As I helped her explore that fear, I saw something deeper. Many of us carry the belief that there's a "right" or "wrong" way to express emotion. That belief can hold us back from being real with our children. It can make us hide the very feelings that help them learn how to be human.

Sharing emotions with our kids isn't about placing our pain on their shoulders. It's about showing them what it looks like to live with feelings. To keep going, even when we're sad, frustrated, or overwhelmed. It's about letting them see that emotions don't need to be hidden. They can sit beside us, and we can still move forward. Those moments become signals, showing children that emotions are not something to fear.

RECOGNITION BEFORE REACTION: IDENTIFYING EMOTIONS

Step one is recognition. Recognition is not only about labeling; it is about noticing. Noticing what is happening on the outside and on the inside.

For children, recognition begins with language. They need help finding words for what they feel. Simple phrases like, "You seem sad," "You look excited," or "Are you feeling frustrated?" give shape to the swirling sensations inside them. These words act like anchors, helping them connect their inner experience to something they can name.

But emotions are not just thoughts. They live in the body first. A tight tummy, a hot face, a lump in the throat, heavy shoulders, a racing heart, these are often the earliest signals that something is happening. When we ask questions like, "Where do you feel that in your body?" or "Does your chest feel tight or your stomach feel wiggly?", we help children connect physical sensations to emotional states. Over time, this builds a bridge between body awareness and emotional awareness.

When your child grunts or cries out while building a Lego tower, it is tempting to jump in with, "Oh, I see you're frustrated." But what if they respond, "No, I'm bored," or "I'm sad"? That is not a minor mislabeling. It is a rupture. It is them trying to claim their inner world for themselves.

Once children can name their emotions, we must let them. Otherwise, we risk replacing their perspective with ours. That is where emotional confusion begins. These early moments teach children whether their internal signals are trustworthy or whether they should defer to someone else's interpretation.

When I first entered the early childhood field, we taught parents to model expressive language for children with developmental delays. We labeled everything—objects, actions, emotions—so children could build vocabulary. But with most typically developing children, if we keep labeling too long, we rob them of the chance to discover their own words.

I'll be honest, I've done this with Connor. When he was younger, I'd say, "You look sad," or "You're frustrated." At that stage, it helped him build language. But as he grew, I realized he needed to name his own emotions and notice his own body cues. Now, instead of telling him, I might say, "Something looks big inside you. What do you think you're feeling?" or "What is your body doing right now?"

Even when he says he's bored, I have to resist the urge to ask, "Are you sure you're not frustrated?" Because children want to please us. If we feed them language, they'll take it. But that is not exploration, that is appeasement. And it means that while they may have already built some of their emotional language, they will sometimes accept what we say over their own opinions to make their caregivers happy. This is the opposite of our goal of helping them build autonomy.

Instead, we explore together. We wonder aloud. We sit with the uncertainty. We ask about their body, their thoughts, and their words. And we feel.

ACKNOWLEDGING EMOTIONS: GIVING FEELINGS ROOM TO EXIST

For children, acknowledgment is the first step toward emotional literacy. When a child cries and hears, "You're OK," the message they absorb is not safety but dismissal. They learn that their emotions should be minimized, that their tears are inconvenient, and that their upset makes others uncomfortable. Over time, this can teach them to distrust their own signals.

Children need to know that their emotions are real, valid, and allowed. When I sat on the cold grocery store floor with Connor, who was sobbing in the frozen food aisle over a toy he couldn't have, the developmental work happening wasn't about the toy at all. It was about Connor learning: *My disappointment is not too big for my mom. My feelings can exist in the open.*

Acknowledgment gives children permission to stay connected to their inner world instead of shutting it down to please others. It teaches them that emotions don't have to be hidden. They can be felt, expressed, and survived.

ACCEPTING EMOTIONS: MODELING EMPATHY

Children don't yet know how to separate their emotions from their behavior. When Connor was two and a half years old and said, "I'm so mad I could punch you," he wasn't threatening violence. He was testing language, trying to match the intensity of his inner storm with words.

By responding with curiosity instead of correction, I gave him space to peel back the layers: anger, then frustration, then sadness. That sequence is the developmental process of emotional differentiation. He was learning that emotions shift, that one feeling can lead to another, and that naming them consistently helps soften the intensity.

Acceptance teaches children that emotions are not dangerous. They are signals. When those signals are met with empathy, children internalize: *My feelings are safe to share. I can trust myself to feel them, and I can trust others to hold them with me.*

PROCESSING EMOTIONS: THE EMOTIONAL STOPGAP MECHANISM

Children cannot flip a switch and turn off their feelings. Their nervous systems are still under construction. What they need is a model that shows them how to slow down the flood.

I call this the **Emotional Stopgap Mechanism**. Imagine a valve in the brain where emotions rush through. You cannot shut it off, but you can slow the flow to a trickle. The stopgap is the pause before the reaction. That pause is where they learn: *I can survive this feeling. I can slow it down.*

Connor first learned Mountain Breathing from a teacher at school, tracing the fingers of one hand with the pointer finger of the other hand while inhaling as he drags the finger up and exhaling as he drags the finger down. Later, I introduced him to the 4-7-8 method of breathing—taking a breath for a count of 4, holding it for a count of 7, exhaling for a count of 8—knowing his love of numbers would make it feel approachable. These practices were not only about helping him calm himself in the moment. They were also developmental tools that helped him regulate his body so his mind could catch up.

The stopgap is not about control. It is about creating space. And for children, that space is where empathy and growth take root.

The Emotional Stopgap is not only a tool for children. Later, in Chapter 15, we will revisit this mechanism from the parent's perspective, exploring how adults can use the same pause to regulate their own emotions and model resilience in real time.

LEANING INTO DISCOMFORT

Children often want to avoid uncomfortable feelings just as much as adults do. But avoidance teaches them that emotions are unsafe. Leaning in teaches them that emotions are survivable.

My client who buried all her feelings under anger illustrates what happens when children never learn this skill. For children, leaning into discomfort means discovering that sadness, frustration, or shame won't swallow them whole. With support, they learn that feelings crest and fall like waves.

That lesson—that emotions can be endured and integrated— is one of the most important developmental milestones of emotional growth.

EMPATHY IN PARENTING: WITNESSING, NOT RESCUING

Empathy means sitting with your child in their emotions. Not fixing. Not judging. Just being there.

One of the hardest moments I faced as a parent was when Connor, overwhelmed by shame and disappointment, screamed that he hated me and wanted to die. To an outsider, it might have looked like defiance. But developmentally, he was drowning in emotion.

By sitting with him, breathing with him, and anchoring in love, I showed him that even in his darkest storm, he was not alone. For a child, that is the deepest form of empathy: *My feelings may overwhelm me, but they don't make me unlovable.*

This is how children learn that connection is possible even in chaos. That lesson becomes the foundation of emotional security. These moments send powerful signals about what love looks like when emotions feel too big.

Sometimes empathy is clearest in the moments we wish had gone differently. One afternoon with Connor stands out as a moment that taught me more about emotional presence than any textbook ever could.

We had gone to pick him up from camp, and the unraveling began before we even reached the car. His counselor pulled us aside to say he had been misbehaving in music theory. He was seven, and the class was not what he expected. They were not playing instruments. They were learning about notes and notation, and he and another child became restless and began running around the room. He heard the counselor's words as a kind of shame, a signal that he had failed at something he did not even want to be doing. I could see the embarrassment settling into his body before he said a word.

Then the day took another turn. The camp barbecue was canceled. His face fell, and he asked me to sit in the backseat with him because he was already feeling the weight of disappointment. I climbed in beside him, hoping my presence would soften the blow. As we drove, we realized the jump-zone place he desperately wanted to visit was not realistic in the time we had left of the day. That final loss was too much for him to hold. His sorrow collapsed into rage.

His breaths became heavy and uneven. His fists tightened. His whole face shifted into fury. When the rage first surged, he began hitting at me, not out of malice but out of desperation. I carefully held his arms to keep us both safe, staying close enough for him to feel my presence without feeling trapped.

Then came the words meant to wound. He screamed that he hated me. Repeated it over and over. But I could see the truth beneath it. He was trying to make me hurt because he was hurting and felt alone in the sea of pain rising inside him. A moment later, the fury gave way to something far heavier. Through sobs, he said he wanted to die.

Tears rolled down my face, not from fear of his words but from the ache of witnessing my child drowning in emotions too big for his body. I stayed steady. I kept my voice soft. I looked directly into his eyes and said, "Well, I do not hate you. I love you, and I always will." I breathed with him, slow and steady, letting him borrow my rhythm until his own began to settle.

What he needed in that moment was not correction or logic. He needed to know he was not alone inside the storm. He needed to feel held, not rescued. He needed to feel loved, not judged.

That moment reminded me that empathy is not about preventing the waves. It is about being the anchor when the waves come.

And it is in these raw, unpolished moments that children learn the deepest truth of emotional security. They learn that even when their feelings overwhelm them, they do not overwhelm us. They learn that connection can survive intensity. They learn that love does not disappear when they lose control.

As I held him through that storm, I realized that empathy is not simply about soothing pain. It is about honoring the person in front of us. And that understanding is at the heart of the Platinum Rule.

THE PLATINUM RULE: EMPATHY IN MOTION

Many of us grew up with the Golden Rule: Treat others as you would like to be treated. It is a beautiful starting point, but it is still centered on the self. It assumes that what I want is what you want, that my needs and preferences are universal.

The **Platinum Rule** was introduced by Dr. Tony Alessandra in the 1990s as a way to expand empathy beyond the self. It says: Treat others how *they* want to be treated. This shift is subtle but profound. It requires us to step outside of our own lens and into someone else's.

For children, this is not just a clever phrase. It is a developmental lifeline. It teaches them that their individuality is real, respected, and worth honoring.

When we practice the Platinum Rule with our children, we are teaching them:

- "My needs matter."
- "My voice is heard."
- "I am not a mini-version of my parent. I am me."

This is not always easy. As parents, we carry our own longings, our own unfinished dreams. We may want our children to love what we love, to follow the paths we once wished we had taken. But when we project those desires onto them, we risk teaching them that love is conditioned on whether they want the same things we do.

I'll admit, I have caught myself doing this with Connor. I wanted him to enjoy something I loved, and when he didn't, I felt that pang of disappointment. But the Platinum Rule reminded me to pivot. Instead of insisting, I asked him what he wanted. And when I honored his choice, I saw something shift in him. He stood taller. He felt seen.

Children who grow up with the Platinum Rule internalize a powerful truth: *I am allowed to be different, and I am still loved.* This is empathy in motion. This is the soil where self-worth grows.

EMOTIONAL GROWTH OVER TIME

Emotional processing evolves with age. A toddler's tantrum, a school-aged child's sobs, a teenager's slammed door—each is developmentally appropriate. What matters is not eliminating these expressions, but walking alongside them.

With Connor, I've already seen the arc: from identifying feelings for him, to letting him name them himself, to now supporting him through more complex storms. Each stage builds on the last. He is learning that emotions are not static. They grow, shift, and become more nuanced over time.

Children need to know that their emotional world will not always feel as overwhelming as it does in the moment. They need to trust that with practice, their capacity to regulate will expand. And they need to see that their parents are not afraid of that growth.

Our job is not to have all the answers. It is to walk alongside them as they learn to feel, name, process, and grow. And as they grow, we grow too.

SIGNALS FOR REFLECTION

- When was the last time I mislabeled my child's emotion instead of letting them name it?
- What physical sensations do I personally notice when I feel overwhelmed, frustrated, or sad? How might sharing those sensations with my child help them learn to identify their own?

- When my child is upset, do I pause to notice what their body is doing before I focus on their behavior?
- When do I soothe my own discomfort instead of acknowledging my child's feelings?
- How do I model the stopgap for my child when I am triggered?
- How often have I been tempted to rescue instead of witness?
- How can I practice the Platinum Rule, honoring my child's unique way of being?
- How am I relearning my own emotional development as I guide theirs?

CLOSING THOUGHTS

Emotions are not a switch you can flip. They are a current that must be felt, acknowledged, and processed.

When we model recognition, acknowledgment, empathy, and the stop-gap method, we give our children the tools to navigate their inner world with courage. We show them that feelings are not dangerous. They are human.

And when we sit with them in their storms—on the grocery store floor, in the back seat of the car, or in the quiet of their room—we are teaching them the most important lesson of all: Emotions are not something to fear or hide. They are something to move through, together.

That is the invisible curriculum of parenting. That is the legacy of emotional security.

Emotional regulation is not about finding one perfect tool. It is about learning how to keep exploring, adapting, and building a toolbox that grows with your child. What soothes them at age five may not work at ten, and eventually they will need to take ownership of that exploration themselves. In the next chapter, we'll look more closely at how to practice these skills in everyday life—through play, presence, and the small social moments that shape emotional fluency.

CHAPTER 11

FOSTERING SOCIAL-EMOTIONAL INTELLIGENCE

How Children Catch What We Feel and Learn Who They Are

FROM EMOTIONAL GROWTH TO SOCIAL FLUENCY

In the last chapter, we explored how emotions are not a switch you can flip, but a current that children must learn to navigate. We learned that inner scaffolding is the foundation. Now we turn outward: how children bring those inner skills into the social world.

Social-emotional intelligence is not built-in. It is learned, practiced, and modeled. And it is caught in the air between us: in the way we breathe, the way we greet strangers, the way we sit beside our children in their storms. These everyday interactions become the signals that teach children how to move through the social world.

SOCIAL-EMOTIONAL SKILLS ARE NOT BUILT-IN

I remember a quiet moment in the hospital with Connor shortly after he was born. I was looking at his beautiful sleeping face, and I was terrified. I knew I would be fine with the logistics of diapers, feeding, and clothing. What terrified me was raising another human while carrying all of my messy emotional reactivity.

No matter how much we think we can control how we feel, the reality is that it is all a gamble if we do not have the tools to respond rather than react. Parenting overwhelm is real: a mixture of fear, awe, and humility. And yet, when we learn to describe emotions, identify them, acknowledge them, and process them, we begin to understand the foundation of social-emotional intelligence.

Children do not arrive fluent in this. They learn it from us. From our tone, our faces, our timing, our tension. From the way we greet the cashier at the grocery store, to the way we respond when juice spills on the couch. Social-emotional intelligence is a lived experience. Children absorb these moments as signals about how people relate, repair, and reconnect.

SOCIAL INTELLIGENCE: WHAT IT REALLY MEANS

Social intelligence is the ability to understand one's own actions and feelings, as well as others', and to learn from them in social settings. It is not innate. It is shaped by experience, by modeling, and by practice.

The idea has been around for more than a century. In 1920, psychologist Edward Thorndike defined social intelligence as "the ability to understand and manage men and women and boys and girls, to act wisely in human relations." Later, Howard Gardner included it in his theory of multiple intelligences as "interpersonal intelligence." Others, like Ross Honeywill, described it as "an aggregated measure of self- and social-awareness." Nicholas Humphrey went even further, suggesting that our capacity for social intelligence is what defines us as human.

Today, one of the most influential frameworks for teaching these skills comes from **CASEL**, the **Collaborative for Academic**, **Social**, and **Emotional Learning**. CASEL identifies five core competencies that form the backbone of social-emotional learning:

- **Self-awareness:** recognizing one's own emotions, thoughts, and values, and understanding how they influence behavior.
- **Self-management:** regulating emotions, thoughts, and behaviors in different situations, including managing stress, controlling impulses, and motivating oneself.
- **Social awareness:** showing understanding and empathy for others, including those from diverse backgrounds and cultures.
- **Relationship skills:** establishing and maintaining healthy and rewarding relationships through communication, listening, cooperation, and conflict resolution.
- **Responsible decision-making:** making ethical, constructive choices about personal and social behavior.

For our children, these competencies are not abstract categories. They are lived, daily practices, and they begin with one thing: connection. Connection is both the internal map that is always evolving and the external guidance they receive from us.

When we model calm, curiosity, and empathy, we are not just teaching manners. We are wiring their brains for social intelligence. We are giving them the tools to navigate friendships, classrooms, and eventually workplaces and families of their own. These modeled moments become the signals that shape how they understand themselves in relation to others.

EMOTIONAL CONTAGION AND MIRRORING: THE VIBE WE BROADCAST

Children are emotional sponges. From the very beginning, their nervous systems are wired to "catch" what we feel. This is not a metaphor, it is biology. Mirror neurons, dispersed across the brain, fire both when we act and when we observe someone else acting. That is why a baby smiles back when you smile, or why your toddler's body stiffens when you tense up.

As we discussed in Chapter 6, this phenomenon is called **emotional contagion**. It is the engine of empathy and the foundation of social learning.

When you are anxious, your infant registers anxiety as if it were their own. When you are distracted, they learn that distraction is normal. When you are joyful, they catch joy.

I once sat with a client who said, "My son is always on edge. He is so reactive." As we talked, she realized she was too. Not because she wanted to be, but because life was overwhelming. And her son was catching it.

When Connor was little, we would go to the grocery store together. I would smile at people, chat with the clerk, say hello to strangers. And Connor? He would do the same. He was learning by watching me.

This is the invisible curriculum of parenting: Your emotional tone is the lesson plan. If you want to raise a child who can name and regulate feelings, you must first model calm, curiosity, and naming. These tones become the signals children use to understand what emotional presence looks like.

And the opposite is also true. I have seen parents walk through stores with their heads down, eyes glued to their phones. No greetings. No engagement. And their children? They mirror that too. They learn that people are background noise. That connection is optional.

In today's world, human connections are harder to come by. We are more digitally connected than ever before, but emotionally we are drifting. We have traded eye contact for screen time, spontaneous play for scheduled activities, and real-world conflict resolution for adult-led interventions. And our children are feeling the loss.

Here is a practical micro-step: Before you enter a public place, take three steady breaths and say aloud, "I am bringing my calm voice. I am going to notice and acknowledge people." Your child will notice you noticing, and start paying closer attention to their environment and all the people in it.

PRACTICING EMOTIONS WHEN THE STAKES ARE LOW

We cannot expect children to regulate during a meltdown if they have never rehearsed regulation in calmer moments. Emotional regulation is like a muscle; it strengthens with practice.

Think of a pianist. They do not only play during concerts. They practice scales, drills, and pieces over and over, so that when the spotlight hits, their fingers know what to do.

Children need the same rehearsal. Board games, chores, playful frustration—these are practice arenas.

Connor, Carl, and I always change the bedding together. It is one of our favorite chores. We put on music, Connor jumps into the pile of blankets, we toss the sheets and pillowcases at each other, we make up silly games. It is fun. It is bonding. And it is practice. Connor is learning cooperation, patience, and joy all at once.

These low-stakes moments matter. They are where children learn to wait their turn, to tolerate frustration, to laugh when things go wrong. They are where they build the muscle memory they will need when the stakes are high—during a meltdown, a conflict with a friend, or a disappointment at school. These moments also teach them to read the subtle signals of social give-and-take.

THE POWER OF NONVERBAL COMMUNICATION AND PRESENCE

Words matter, but nonverbal signals are absorbed first. Eye contact, facial expression, touch, pacing, and what I call "focused presence" are the connectors that wire a child's social brain.

When parents hide behind screens and offer only a disembodied voice, infants literally lose a core learning stimulus. Lack of face-to-face input is emotionally impoverishing in the same way isolation is for adults.

Presence is not about having the right phrases. It is about showing up visibly and steadily. A parent who pauses to meet a child's eyes during a meltdown teaches that feelings are seen and survivable. Presence de-escalates the nervous system faster than logic.

I once had a friend who went through a painful divorce. She told me later that what helped her most was not the advice people gave, but the one friend who simply sat with her on the couch, held her hand, and said nothing. "She didn't try to fix it," my friend said. "She just looked at me, and I felt like I wasn't alone." That is the power of presence.

I have been told many times that I carry a "nurturing presence." I have walked into rooms where people later said they felt calmer just because I was there. I wasn't doing anything extraordinary—I was simply grounded, attentive, and open. That quiet steadiness shifted the atmosphere. People leaned in, softened, and matched the tone. Children notice this too. They learn that presence is not only comfort, it is influence.

Children need both of these lessons. They need to experience presence as comfort—the steady hand that says, "I am with you." And they need to see presence as influence, the way one person's calm can ripple outward and change the atmosphere for everyone. These nonverbal cues become some of the strongest signals they internalize about safety and connection.

When we meet our child's eyes, slow our breath, and stay close, we are teaching them that emotions are survivable and that connection is possible even in chaos. And when they see us bring calm into a room, they learn that their presence has power too.

THE DANGER OF DIGITAL DISCONNECTION

Screens are not the enemy, but they can steal something precious: the chance to read real faces, hear real tone, and feel real connection.

We once had a toddler in our system who barely spoke. His parents were kind but rarely engaged in conversation with him. The child mirrored that silence. Language is caught. Emotion is caught. Without rich, expressive human interaction, children lack the tools to navigate the social world.

Social-emotional intelligence grows in real social soil. Screens can simulate people, places, and things, but they cannot replace the messy, richly textured learning of in-person connection through play.

This is not about banning technology. It is about balance. It is about remembering that children need to practice reading faces, hearing tone, and feeling presence. Without that, their social muscles atrophy.

LET THEM PLAY WITHOUT US

One of the most powerful ways to build social-emotional intelligence is through peer play. Not adult-led activities. Not structured activities. Just kids, figuring it out.

Unstructured, unsupervised play builds peer-to-peer negotiation, rule-making, and conflict repair. But we have lost much of that. We have replaced free play with supervised outings. We have stepped in to solve every conflict. And in doing so, we have robbed our children of the chance to learn how to negotiate, compromise, and repair.

When children can experience a friend's perspective on why they should play tag instead of exploring the woods, they find ways to compromise so everyone gets a little of what they want. But when adults step in to stop the arguments and provide direction, children assume only adults know how to repair conflict. This results in them solidifying their own perspective without the opportunity to see another's.

I remember watching Connor and his friends play a game together. They were arguing over rules, shouting, disagreeing. I started to step in but quickly stopped myself. They needed to work it out. And they did.

That is social-emotional learning. In real time. In real relationships. These moments teach children to read the signals of peer dynamics, not just adult cues.

A quick note: Unsupervised play changes with age and context. Recently, some states introduced "Reasonable Childhood Independence" laws to protect families who allow older kids low-risk freedoms such as walking a short block or playing with nearby friends. That legal language can feel worrying, but it does not replace common sense. A ten-year-old playing with neighbors is not the same as a toddler left alone in a store, and experts weigh age, location, and nearby supervision when they assess whether a situation was neglectful.

We can use a simple rule of thumb to test a hypothetical situation. Unsupervised play means age-appropriate independence in a reasonably safe setting; neglect means placing a child where substantial harm is likely. If you are unsure, pause, check local guidance, and try a small, supervised step toward more freedom rather than one big test. Organizations such as Let Grow (letgrow.org) offer practical toolkits and community programs that can help families balance safety, local rules, and gradual independence.

PRACTICAL TOOLS TO FOSTER SOCIAL EMOTIONAL INTELLIGENCE

- **Emotional check-ins:** Once a day, ask your child, "What is one feeling you had today?" Model your own: "I felt proud when I finished that task." Let them name theirs without correction.
- **Eye contact moments:** During meals, bedtime, or transitions, pause and make eye contact. Say: "I see you. I am here." Let your gaze be the connector.
- **Cooperative games:** Play board games, make up rules, let them lead. Use conflict as a teaching moment: "What do you think we should do now?"
- **Breathing techniques:** Try Mountain Breathing or "4-7-8 Breathing" together. Use it before school, after a meal, after meltdowns, or during transitions.
- **Narrate your inner world:** Say aloud: "I am feeling over-

whelmed, so I am going to take a breath." This models emotional literacy and regulation.

- **Unstructured play time:** Create weekly windows for unsupervised play. Let children argue, negotiate, and find resolution in their interactions without adult intervention.

SIGNALS FOR REFLECTION

- When was the last time you made eye contact with your child during a routine moment? What shifted in them—and in you—when you did?
- When was the last time you modeled an emotion rather than corrected one? How did your child respond?
- What emotional signals are you broadcasting without words? Pause and ask yourself: Are they catching calm or are they catching hurry and stress?
- Where in your child's life can you create more unsupervised play? Give yourself permission to step back for two extra minutes before intervening and notice what happens.
- How do you respond when your child misreads a situation? Do you correct, or do you explore with curiosity? Try asking, "What made you think that?" before offering your perspective.
- What is one way you can model emotional regulation this week? Choose a small, ordinary moment—folding laundry, cooking dinner, walking the dog—and turn it into practice.
- Where could you swap ten minutes of screen time for ten minutes of face-to-face connection? Notice how even a small shift changes the emotional climate of your home.
- The next time your child is upset, resist the urge to explain or fix. Instead, slow your breath, meet their eyes, and simply stay. What do you notice in their body language when you do this?

CLOSING THOUGHTS

Social-emotional intelligence is not taught in lectures. It is caught in the quiet moments. In the way we breathe. In the way we listen. In the way we sit beside our children when they are melting down and say, "I am here."

When we commit to modeling it, not perfectly but consistently, we give our children the tools to thrive. Not just in school. Not just in relationships. But in life.

If Chapter 11 is about the air we breathe together—the emotions children recognize and carry from us and from their peers—then Chapter 12 is about the roots beneath the surface. This is where belonging takes shape, identity begins to form, and children learn not just how to connect with others, but who they are within those connections.

SELF-ESTEEM VS IMAGE ESTEEM

The Compass Within and the Mirror Without

THE GOLDEN NUGGET

Self-esteem is how we feel and what we think of ourselves. Image esteem is *not* what others think of us, but what we *believe* others think of us, and the *weight* we give that belief.

Think of it this way: Self-esteem is the compass inside your child. Image esteem is the funhouse mirror they hold up to themselves, distorted by imagined judgments. These two forces send very different signals about who they are and where their worth comes from.

This distinction is the heartbeat of this chapter. It is the difference between a child who feels grounded in their own worth, and one who constantly scans the room for approval. Between a teen who can say "no" with clarity and one who says "yes" to avoid rejection. Between a child who can survive your absence and one who feels lost without your gaze.

When I was a child, I had a friend who barely said a word. She was kind, but so quiet that teachers often passed her over. When she did raise her hand, she spoke so softly that teachers grew impatient and called on someone else.

Later I learned that her mother had told her not to call attention to herself because her voice was "annoying." It took years of therapy, support, and intentional moments of spotlight before she finally found her real voice.

I learned then that self-esteem is not built in grand gestures. It is built in the moments we choose to see our children clearly and speak to their worth as if it is sacred. Because it is.

THE PSYCHOLOGY OF SELF-ESTEEM

Self-esteem is not just a feeling. It is the lens through which children interpret the world, regulate their emotions, and form relationships. Built through attachment, autonomy, and reflection, it becomes the scaffolding for resilience, identity, and moral development.

SELF-ESTEEM AS AN INTERNAL COMPASS

Self-esteem is the inner compass children use to decide: *Am I capable? Am I enough?*

One client told me about her son, Jonah, who was excited to build a wind turbine for the school science fair. For days he worked in the living room, cutting cardboard, twisting wires, asking endless questions. The night before the fair, he suddenly refused to go. "It's dumb," he said. "My project isn't good enough."

His mom told me later that her first instinct was frustration. She wanted to say, "You worked so hard on this, don't throw it away." But underneath that frustration was fear. She worried that if he quit now, he would learn to quit whenever he felt insecure. She worried that her own perfectionism had seeped into him.

Instead, she took a breath and said, "You don't have to be perfect. Trying something new and sticking with it is what matters. You're learning. That's brave."

The next morning, Jonah went. He did not win, but he stood proudly beside his project. His compass had shifted from shame to courage.

Psychologist Carol Dweck's research on growth mindset shows that children with healthy self-esteem see mistakes as stepping stones, while those with fragile esteem see them as cliffs.

ATTACHMENT THEORY AND THE ROOTS OF ESTEEM

John Bowlby's attachment theory shows that secure attachment lays the foundation for self-esteem. When caregivers respond with warmth and reliability, children internalize safety and self-worth.

The day that Connor looked at me and said, "You'll always be here, in my heart," he wasn't just being poetic. He was working something out. He was asking: "If you're not right next to me, do I still have you?"

That sentence was his answer. It was the moment he realized that love can be carried inside. That even when I walk out of the room, he doesn't lose me. He can hold me in his heart as a steady presence.

For me, it was more than touching. It was evidence that he had built an inner secure base—the invisible anchor that allows a child to explore the world without fear of losing connection.

And it struck me because many people I know, myself included, didn't grow up with that. Absence in their childhood often felt like abandonment. For Connor, absence could feel like presence. That's the difference secure attachment makes. These early experiences become the signals children use to decide whether they are safe, seen, and held.

Mary Ainsworth's "Strange Situation" studies showed that securely attached children explore more confidently and recover more quickly from stress because their inner compass points to safety.

SOCIAL COMPARISON AND THE EMERGENCE OF IMAGE ESTEEM

Around ages seven to eight, children begin comparing themselves to peers. This is when image esteem emerges, the sense of how they believe others perceive them. This is the moment when a child who once felt proud can suddenly feel "less than" in the presence of someone else's skill.

One of my part time Early Intervention practitioners, who taught during the day, once shared a story from her classroom that stayed with me. One of her students had proudly finished a drawing of a rocket ship. He had worked on it for days, carefully coloring the flames and shading the windows. When he held it up, his face lit with pride. But then he glanced at the child next to him, whose drawing had more detail and sharper lines. In an instant, his shoulders dropped. He folded his paper and shoved it into his backpack. The rocket had not changed. Only his imagined reflection in someone else's eyes had.

That is the power of social comparison. It can shrink a child's joy in seconds. These moments send potent signals about whether their worth is stable, or dependent on someone else's performance.

Psychologist Leon Festinger described this as Social Comparison Theory, which explains how we measure ourselves against others to evaluate our own worth. For children, this is not just about skill. It is about identity.

My practitioner reflected on how often she saw this dynamic play out. A child who was once enthusiastic about reading aloud would suddenly clam up after hearing another student read with more fluency. A child who loved math puzzles would stop raising their hand after noticing a peer solve problems faster. The comparison was not about ability alone. It was about how they believed others now saw them.

This is the work of parenting and teaching in the age of comparison. We cannot remove the mirrors, but we can help children interpret what they see. We can remind them that their worth is not measured against someone else's accomplishment, it is rooted in their own effort, growth, and joy.

COGNITIVE DEVELOPMENT AND SELF-EVALUATION

By adolescence, children can reflect on their own thoughts and feelings. But without emotional safety, reflection can turn into rumination. Rumination is the mental equivalent of getting stuck in quicksand.

One colleague told me about her daughter, Maya, who came home in tears after not being invited to a sleepover. At first, she seemed fine. But later that night, her mom found her curled up in bed, whispering the same things over and over: "Why didn't they invite me?" "Did I do something wrong?" "Maybe nobody likes me."

Instead of moving through those thoughts, Maya replayed them endlessly. Each pass dug the groove deeper. Rumination feels like being trapped in a mental spin cycle: the same clothes, the same water, endlessly churning.

Here is what is happening in the brain. The "default mode

network," the system that turns on when our mind wanders, becomes overactivated. Instead of wandering toward curiosity or imagination, it circles back to self-criticism and what-ifs. The brain keeps pressing "replay" instead of "next track."

That is why practices like mindfulness, journaling, or even physical movement are so powerful. They interrupt the loop. They give the brain a new channel to follow, teaching kids that thoughts are not facts and that they can choose to step out of the spin cycle.

For Maya, her mom sat beside her and said, "I can't answer why they didn't invite you. But I can sit with you while you feel this." That moment did not erase the pain, but it gave Maya something more important: the experience of not being alone inside the loop. Over time, with gentle coaching, she began to write her feelings down instead of replaying them in her head. Slowly, she learned that naming the thought was the first step to loosening its grip.

NEUROBIOLOGY OF SELF-WORTH

Self-esteem is not only psychological, it is also biological. The brain and body are in constant dialogue, shaping how children experience their own worth. The prefrontal cortex helps with self-assessment and impulse control. The limbic system processes emotional feedback. The stress-response system, known as the HPA axis, learns over time whether the world is survivable or overwhelming.

One mom told me about her son, Daniel, who froze every time he had to read aloud in class. His face flushed, his hands shook, and afterward he would say, "I'm just bad at this." What was happening inside him was not laziness or lack of intelligence. His nervous system was flooding with cortisol, the stress hormone, and his body was bracing for danger.

At home, his parents began practicing short breathing exercises with him before homework. They would sit together, place a hand on their bellies, and count slowly as they inhaled and exhaled. At first, Daniel resisted. But over time, he noticed that his heart slowed and his thoughts cleared. One day, after reading aloud without stumbling, he whispered, "I felt calmer, like I could think again."

That moment was not just psychological progress. It was neurobiology in action. His parasympathetic nervous system, the body's natural calming system, had been activated. His brain was learning that stress could be managed, that fear did not have to control him, and that he could recover.

This is what attuned caregiving does. It literally rewires the brain. When children receive consistent, supportive responses, their stress-response system learns to regulate. Cortisol spikes lessen. Resilience pathways strengthen. The body begins to believe: *I can survive this. I can try again.*

And when children internalize that belief, they carry it into every challenge. They do not crumble at the first sign of difficulty. They know, in their bones, that they are capable of returning to balance. That is the biology of self-worth.

THE SOCIAL MEDIA MIRROR

Social media often functions like a hall of mirrors: curated, filtered, and performative. Children step inside and suddenly their reflection is multiplied, stretched, and distorted. They begin to measure their worth in accumulated "friends," "likes", views, and comments. They compare their behind-the-scenes to someone else's highlight reel, forgetting that what they are seeing is not reality but a carefully staged performance.

I remember one mom telling me about her daughter, Louise, who had just returned from a trip to the Grand Canyon. For days, she had been in awe, pointing out every layer of rock, every shift of light, every echo in the canyon walls. She came home glowing, her joy spilling over as she posted photos of herself standing at the edge, arms wide, hair wild in the wind.

A few hours later, the comments rolled in. Most were kind, with friends saying how beautiful the canyon looked and how happy she seemed. But tucked between them were daggers: "You look like a moron." "Ugly." "Take it down before someone's eyes are permanently damaged."

For a thirteen-year-old girl, those words could have been shattering. And the truth is, for many children, they are.

When self-esteem is fragile, one cruel comment can outweigh ninety kind ones. It is like pouring ink into a glass of water. The whole thing feels tainted. A child with shaky self-worth will ruminate, replaying the insult until it drowns out the memory of joy. They may delete the post, question their appearance, or vow never to show up so authentically again.

But Louise surprised her mom. She read the comments, rolled her eyes, and said, "Well, that's a 'them' issue." She left the post up, preserving her joy.

That moment revealed something powerful. Louise's self-esteem was strong enough to filter the noise. She could see the cruelty for what it was, a reflection of the commenter, not of her.

Neuroscience helps explain why this is so hard for many kids. Every 'like' on social media triggers a small release of dopamine, the brain's feel-good chemical. It is the same system that lights up when we eat chocolate or hear our favorite song. For children with shaky self-esteem, this can become addictive.

They begin to chase the next hit of approval, confusing visibility with value.

But here is the deeper truth: Our children are watching us in these mirrors too. They notice how we post, how we react to comments, how we measure ourselves against others. If we sigh when a photo does not get enough likes, or if we curate our lives to look shinier than they are, we are teaching them that image esteem matters more than self-esteem.

So, the question is not only, "How do I help my child navigate social media?" It is also, "What reflection of worth am I modeling in my own digital mirror?"

Because when we post from joy, not from a hunger to be seen, we show our children that their worth is not up for public vote.

HOW TO FOSTER SELF-ESTEEM

Self-esteem is not built in grand gestures. It is built in quiet moments, when children feel safe enough to be messy, honest, and unsure. Healthy parenting guidelines will help facilitate positive self-esteem in children.

CREATE PERSONAL BOUNDARIES

Boundaries teach children that their body, time, and emotions are sacred. When we model this by honoring our own needs without guilt, we show them that self-respect is not selfish. It is the foundation of healthy connection.

CLARIFY CORE VALUES

Children need anchors that go deeper than performance. Ask your child questions like, "What matters most to you? What kind of friend do you want to be?" These conversations help them see that identity is not about grades or trophies, but about the kind of human being they are becoming.

TEACH HEALTHY COPING STRATEGIES

Offer tools, not fixes. Breathwork, journaling, movement, and naming emotions all give children ways to regulate without shame. In our home, we use "debriefs," calm reflections after intense moments. These are not lectures. They are gentle pauses that tell a child: You are safe enough to look at what just happened and learn from it.

PROVIDE A REAL SAFE SPACE

Children need a place to say, "I messed up," or "I feel jealous," without fear of rejection. When we hold space for their hardest emotions, we show them that love stays steady, even when they're not at their best. Emotional permission is the assurance that their feelings won't cost them connection. It tells a child, "You are safe to feel, and I will walk with you through it." When we create this space with our children, and teach them how to appropriately create it for themselves, they bring that sanctuary with them, like a "mental security blanket" for the hard moments.

But we must be clear: A true safe space is not the same as a bubble. As Dr. Jonathan Haidt and the Let Grow movement remind us, growth requires exposure to manageable risks and struggles. Shielding children from every discomfort may feel protective, but it leaves them unprepared. Just as the immune system strengthens by meeting germs, the emotional system strengthens by meeting setbacks, disappointments, and even criticism.

A healthy safe space is not about removing every hard thing.

It is about creating a secure base where children can process those hard things without shame. It is the difference between saying, "I will never let you fall," and saying, "When you fall, I will be here to support you as you learn how to get back up on your own."

As children grow, it is not up to others to provide these spaces for them. They must learn where and when to carve them out for themselves, without encroaching on other people's environments. On a college campus, for example, the purpose is to learn, usually new things you do not already know. Expanding your knowledge means you may hear ideas that unsettle you, challenge your assumptions, or even activate a strong emotional response. That discomfort is not a sign of danger. It is a sign of growth.

Growth does not happen in a bubble. Leaning into discomfort allows us to dive deeper into our own choices, experiences, and knowledge gaps. It widens our comfort zone. And when children learn this balance early, that they can feel safe enough to process their emotions while still facing life's hurdles, the world feels less frightening. They step into it with more confidence, knowing they can handle both the joy and the struggle.

WHEN TO BE CONCERNED

It's important to watch for signs that your child's image esteem may be eclipsing their self-esteem. For example:

- They constantly seek external validation.
- They fear being alone or unseen.
- They change themselves to fit in.
- They struggle to make decisions without approval from others.

If these patterns persist and interfere with daily life or relationships, it's time to gently intervene. Not with correction, but with connection. Ask questions. Reflect back their strengths. Remind them of who they are when no one's watching. Sometimes, it's necessary to consider reaching out to a trusted teacher, coach or clinician for guidance.

Self-esteem isn't one-size-fits-all. It's not just about how a child feels in social settings—whether they feel liked, accepted, or confident around peers. There's another layer, often quieter but just as powerful: the perfectionist's self-esteem, which is tied not to relationships, but to performance.

Take Connor, for example. He's not usually worried about what others think of him socially. He's usually very comfortable in a group. But when he gets a math problem wrong or loses a game he thought he should win, something shifts. His self-talk becomes harsh. His body tightens. He spirals into overwhelm, even rage, not because someone judged him, but because he judged himself.

This is the perfectionist's trap:

- Mistakes feel like identity threats.
- Effort feels meaningless unless it leads to mastery.
- Failure isn't feedback—it's proof of inadequacy.

While social self-esteem asks, "Am I accepted?" a perfectionist's self-esteem asks, "Am I enough when I'm not perfect?"

Children like Connor often internalize a belief that their worth is conditional, based on achievement, correctness, or control. They may:

- Avoid trying new things unless they're sure they'll succeed.
- Shut down emotionally when they make mistakes.

- Struggle to regulate their nervous system after perceived failure.
- Feel shame, not just disappointment.

With steady support, children can learn to loosen this grip. In our family, we have been working on this together, along with the wonderful professionals who support our son outside our home, and we are starting to see small but meaningful shifts. His self-talk softens more quickly now, and he recovers from mistakes with a little more ease. Progress in this area takes time, but watching him grow has been a quiet joy.

This isn't just about high standards, it's about fragile self-worth. And it's often rooted in early experiences where praise was tied to performance, or where emotional safety felt contingent on "getting it right." It could even have been just one single moment that he absorbed differently than it was intended, which ultimately stuck with him.

REBUILDING THE COMPASS

To support children in these moments, we must help them feel secure in failure. That means:

- Modeling self-compassion when we mess up;
- Praising effort and recovery, not just results;
- Teaching a child to name feelings and breathe through storms;
- Reminding them: You are not your mistake. You are not your score. You are not your win.

Self-esteem, in this context, becomes an internal compass, not a scoreboard. It helps a child navigate setbacks with resilience, rather than collapse. It teaches them to persist with purpose, even when the path isn't perfect. These moments send powerful signals about where worth truly lives.

DEVELOPMENTAL TOUCHPOINTS

Self-esteem grows differently at each stage of childhood.

- **Early childhood:** Focus on emotional naming and bodily autonomy. Celebrate effort over outcome.
- **Middle childhood:** Introduce values and boundaries. Let them choose clothes, friends, and interests.
- **Adolescence:** Normalize identity exploration. Encourage critical thinking. Offer mentorship, not micromanagement.

THE GARDENER'S ROLE

Self-esteem is not fixed. It grows through rupture and repair, reflection and resilience. You are the gardener. You do not control the weather, but you tend the soil. You create the conditions where growth is possible, even when storms come. The signals you send through presence, boundaries, and empathy become the nutrients that help worth take root.

SIGNALS FOR REFLECTION

- When my child makes a mistake, do I respond with curiosity or correction?
- Have I praised effort, resilience, and emotional growth, or mostly outcomes and achievements?
- Have I ever unintentionally joked about their body, voice, or style—and how might that have landed?

- What do my facial expressions say when my child shares something vulnerable?
- Do I make eye contact when my child is speaking, or do I multitask?
- When they dress creatively or differently, do I celebrate it, or subtly steer them toward "acceptable" choices?
- How do I speak about my own body, mistakes, or emotions in front of my child?
- Do I allow myself to be seen in imperfection, or do I hide my struggles?
- Do I expect my child to be "good" at things quickly, or do I normalize learning curves?
- Am I more comfortable when my child is quiet and agreeable, or when they assert themselves?
- Does my child feel safe coming to me when they are ashamed, embarrassed, or unsure?
- Have I created space for them to express anger, sadness, or disappointment without fear of rejection?
- Am I rescuing my child from struggle, or supporting them in learning how to rise from it?

CLOSING THOUGHTS

Self-esteem is the compass within. Image esteem is the mirror without. When we strengthen the compass, our children can navigate storms with steadiness. When we overemphasize the mirror, they lose themselves in distortions.

But self-esteem does not grow in isolation. It grows the way a garden does, through steady tending. We cannot control every storm, every drought, or every harsh season our children will face. What we can do is prepare the soil, water it with consistency, and prune with gentleness. We can create the conditions where resilience takes root and where worth is not dependent on the weather.

And when we tend the soil well, our children carry that strength with them. They step into the world not empty-handed, but rooted, resilient, and equipped with inner resources they can draw on when life feels uncertain.

The next step is to explore what draws them forward: the sunlight that pulls growth out of the soil of self-esteem. Self-esteem is not a structure poured in concrete; it is a living system. Even if early storms leave scars, steady tending and new sunlight can restore growth. At every stage, children and adults alike can strengthen their compass and re-root their worth.

CHAPTER 13

WHEN YOUR CHILD SAYS "I CAN'T"

From "I Can't" to "I Can Try"

MORE THAN TWO LITTLE WORDS

How many times have you heard your child say those two little words, "I can't"? If you're like many parents, it's enough to make you want to bang your head against the wall. Whether it's homework, tying shoes, cleaning up, or trying something new, "I can't" can feel like a brick wall between you and your child's cooperation.

But here's the truth: "I can't" almost never means what we think it means. It's not laziness. It's not defiance. It's not even always about ability. More often than not, "I can't" is a signal. It's a clue pointing us toward what's really going on inside our child.

And when we learn to decode it, we unlock one of the most powerful tools in parenting: **motivation.**

THE THREE ROOTS OF "I CAN'T"

When a child says, "I can't," it usually comes from one of three places:

1. **Lack of knowledge:** They simply don't know how yet. Think of a child learning to tie their shoes for the first time. They don't even know what "tying" means, let alone how to loop, swoop, and pull. "I can't" here really means, "I don't know how."
2. **Lack of practice:** They understand the concept, but they haven't had enough chances to try. A child may know what subtraction is, but until they've worked through problems themselves, they can't do it. "I can't" here means, "I haven't practiced enough to feel capable."
3. **Lack of desire (motivation):** Sometimes, "I can't" is really, "I don't want to." This is where motivation comes in. Maybe they know how to do their homework, but they'd rather be outside. Maybe they've cleaned their room before, but today they'd rather play.

As parents, our job is to pause and ask: Which one is it this time? Knowledge? Practice? Or motivation?

WHY MOTIVATION MATTERS

This is why motivation matters. It's the bridge between "I can't" and "I can." Without it, even the most capable child will resist. With it, even the hardest tasks become possible.

And here's the bigger picture: Motivation is not just about getting chores done or homework finished. It's about raising children who know how to make decisions for themselves, who can cooperate without being forced, and who grow into adults that lead their own lives with confidence.

If we only ever push, punish, or bribe, we raise children who wait for someone else to tell them what to do. But if we learn to tap into what motivates them, we raise children who can say, "I choose to do this." That's the foundation of autonomy and competence. It also teaches them to trust the internal signals that guide their choices.

INTRINSIC VS. EXTRINSIC MOTIVATION

Motivation comes in two forms:

- **Intrinsic motivation:** Doing something because it lights you up inside. A child who loves music doesn't need reminders to sing. A child who loves building will spend hours with Legos. This is the "I want to" energy.
- **Extrinsic motivation:** Doing something because of an outside reason—because it's required, expected, or rewarded. A child may not *want* to do math homework, but they know they'll get screen time afterward. This is the "I should" energy.

Both have their place. But intrinsic motivation tends to be stronger and more enduring, longer-lasting, and more joyful. Our role as parents is to notice what leads our children to light up in life. And then, whenever possible, pair those intrinsic motivators with the tasks they resist. When we can pair daily tasks with a child's interests, cooperation grows.

OPTIMAL VS. SUBOPTIMAL MOTIVATION

Not all motivation is created equal.

- **Suboptimal motivation** is when we rely on threats, punishments, or guilt. "Do your homework or no TV." "Clean your room or you're grounded." These tactics may work in the short term, but they erode cooperation, trust, and connection over time.
- **Optimal motivation** is when we connect the task to something meaningful or enjoyable for the child. For example:
  - Pairing homework with music breaks.
  - Letting a child jump on the trampoline for two minutes after ten minutes of math.
  - Allowing them to color between writing assignments.

One night, my son had a long writing assignment. He hates handwriting because it hurts his joints. So we made a deal; after each line he wrote, he could color a holiday cookie with food-coloring markers. Line, color. Line, color. Suddenly, the dreaded task became bearable.

Here's the fascinating part: coloring and handwriting use different fine motor skills. These differences are consistent with occupational therapy observations about fine-motor demands. Writing requires a structured pencil grip, while coloring can be looser and more playful. To him, it felt like a break, even though both involved his hands.

Did it make sense to me at first? Not really. But it worked for him. And that's the point. Motivation doesn't have to make sense to us, it only has to work for the child.

THE ROLE OF CURIOSITY AND EXPLORATION

Curiosity is the birthplace of motivation. Humans are born curious, rolling over to reach for a toy, putting everything in their mouths, asking endless "why" questions. But over time, curiosity can get shut down when we tell children what they should like, what they must do, or what's "worthwhile."

Even adults can lose touch with curiosity. There were times when my husband, a true introvert, would say he felt bored but didn't know what he wanted to do. I used to suggest activities, but nothing stuck. Eventually, I encouraged him to follow his own little "I wonder..." moments. Over time, he discovered new interests simply by paying attention to those sparks.

If adults need reminders to follow curiosity, imagine how much more children need space and guidance to discover what lights them up.

One mom I worked with told me, "I don't know what my daughter likes. She just likes whatever I tell her to like." Now, this doesn't mean she was doing anything wrong. What she realized was that she had been passing along all the things she enjoyed, rather than exploring the world with her daughter. So, I asked her to give her daughter choices instead of instructions: "Do you want to draw, dance, or play outside?" Within a week, a pattern emerged. Her daughter chose drawing every time. Suddenly, this mom could see one of her child's true motivators.

As parents, one of our greatest responsibilities is to create space to simply watch our children. When we step back and observe, we begin to notice where their curiosity naturally leads, rather than always steering them with what we already know. And here's the beautiful part: Sometimes their discoveries open doors we never would have walked through ourselves. They may uncover interests, passions, or joys that not only light them up, but also bring unexpected delight into our own lives. In giving them room to explore, we often find our world expanding right alongside theirs.

That same client recently shared that her daughter loves exploring the grocery store, especially finding new foods to bring home. Now they've made it a weekly ritual to try at least one new dish together.

Moments like these remind us that when we step back and let curiosity lead, our children often show us not only what motivates them, but also new ways of bringing joy and discovery into family life. Their explorations become our invitations to grow alongside them.

When we allow curiosity, we discover what lights our children up, and when we know what lights them up, we can use it to help them through the tasks that don't. These moments reveal the signals that point toward their natural sources of energy and joy.

WHY MOTIVATION BUILDS COOPERATION

Humans aren't robots. We don't just do what we're told; we make choices. And children need practice making choices if they're going to grow into adults who can lead their own lives.

If we always say, "Do it because I said so," we raise children who wait for someone else to decide for them. But if we say, "Let's figure out what helps you want to do this," we raise children who learn to cooperate from their own will.

That's the difference between raising followers and raising leaders.

One chilly morning, my son didn't want to get out of bed. I suggested he try getting dressed under the covers, a trick I used as a child to stay warm while getting dressed on chilly mornings.

He tried it, but quickly became uncomfortable because he also needed to use the bathroom.

At first, he wanted to blame me: "You made me do this!" But I reminded him, "I didn't make you. You chose to try it. And now you know what your body needs first."

That moment was about more than pajamas. It was about learning to listen to his own needs, to make decisions for himself, and to speak up. That's motivation in action, paired with autonomy. It also teaches him to trust the internal signals that guide his choices.

CASTING FORWARD: WHY THIS MATTERS IN THE LONG TERM

When children don't learn to connect with their own motivators, they risk growing into adults who:

- Stay in jobs they hate because they're "good at it" or it pleases others.
- Stay in unhealthy relationships because they don't know how to choose differently.
- Or, on the flip side, avoid responsibility altogether because they only ever did what they wanted, never what was needed.

Neither extreme is healthy. The sweet spot is balance: doing what's required *and* what lights us up. That's what healthy motivation teaches.

STRATEGIES FOR PARENTS

- **Observe:** Watch what your child gravitates toward naturally. Write it down if you need to.

- **Pair:** Connect suboptimal tasks (homework, chores) with intrinsic motivators (music, movement, art, games).
- **Offer choices:** Instead of dictating, give options. "Do you want to do homework at the table or on the floor?"
- **Stay curious:** Ask, "What would make this easier for you?"
- **Model it:** Let your child see you pairing your own have-to list with motivators. For example, "I don't love doing dishes, but I put on my favorite podcast while I do them."

SIGNALS FOR REFLECTION

- When my child says, "I can't," do I tend to hear it as defiance, laziness, lack of ability, or do I see what's beneath this phrase? What signal might that send about how I view their effort or worth?
- Growing up, how did my parents or caregivers respond when I said, "I can't"? Did I feel encouraged, dismissed, or pressured, and how might that still echo in the way I respond today?
- Have I ever unintentionally sent the message that my child's intrinsic motivators (their natural joys and curiosities) don't matter as much as the "shoulds" or "musts"? How might I begin to honor those motivators more fully?
- When I rely on suboptimal motivators (threats, punishments, guilt), what unspoken signal does that send about cooperation? Does it teach compliance, or does it nurture autonomy?
- Do I model for my child how I motivate myself through tasks I don't enjoy? What unspoken lessons am I teaching them about resilience, curiosity, and pairing joy with responsibility?
- If I imagine my child as an adult one day, what signals do I hope they carry forward about their ability to say, "I can," even when something feels hard? What signals do I want to stop passing down?

CLOSING THOUGHTS

"I can't" is not the end of the story. It's the beginning of a conversation. When we pause to ask what's really behind those words—knowledge, practice, or motivation—we open the door to cooperation, confidence, and growth.

And while I can't promise you'll never hear "I can't" again, I can promise that how you respond will change everything. Instead of frustration or power struggles, you'll begin to see opportunities: opportunities to teach, to connect, and to guide your child toward discovering their own strength. Over time, those small shifts add up. You'll hear more "I can try," more "I'll figure it out," and eventually, more "I can."

Because in the end, motivation isn't just about getting through homework or chores. It's about raising children who believe in their own ability to learn, to grow, and to choose. That belief is a gift they will carry with them for the rest of their lives.

CHAPTER 14

TO CONTROL OR NOT TO CONTROL?

A Parent's Perspective on Boundaries, Autonomy, and Connection

THE INVISIBLE TURNING POINT

There is a moment in every parent's journey that feels almost invisible, yet it changes everything. It is the moment when the desire to protect collides with the need to release. You feel it when your child pulls their hand away for the first time, when they say "no" with conviction, or when they look at you with eyes that say, "I've got this." In that instant, you realize that parenting is not about holding on tighter. It is about learning how to let go with wisdom, grace, and trust. These moments are signals, subtle cues that your child is stepping into their own becoming.

There is a quiet paradox in parenting: We want our children to grow into independent, capable people, yet we often struggle with the discomfort of letting go. Control is one of the hardest concepts for parents to navigate. We want to protect, guide, and shape, but we also know that autonomy is essential for growth.

This chapter is not about why children need autonomy. That was the focus of Chapter 7. Instead, this is about us, the parents. It is about how we wrestle with our own fears, judgments, and impulses to control, and how we can learn to create boundaries that empower rather than restrict.

THE PARENT'S INNER STRUGGLE WITH CONTROL

When we try to avoid being authoritarian, we often swing too far toward permissiveness. We want to be kind, flexible, and understanding, but without structure, children feel unmoored. On the other hand, when we fear losing control, we can become rigid, reactive, or inconsistent.

The truth is, children don't need us to be perfect. They need us to be steady. They need us to create rules that make sense, boundaries that are consistent, and a family environment where accountability is shared.

But here is the hard part: Before we can create those boundaries, we have to face our own discomfort with letting go. That discomfort often shows up as internal signals of fear, urgency, or overprotection.

A STORY FROM THE FIELD AND THE HEART

One day at a carnival, Connor made fast friends with another child. They were laughing and playing until the child began smacking Connor. At first, it seemed playful. Connor laughed and told him to stop. The child did not stop. Connor grew firmer, more annoyed, and told him again. I watched, waiting to see how he would handle it.

When Connor finally looked to me for help, I glanced at the child's mother. She was busy taking pictures of her other child and typing on her phone. She hadn't noticed a thing. So I stepped in. I told the child firmly that hitting was not OK and that if it continued, they could not play together. That worked for a while, but when it happened again, I said, "No, we are done now," then took Connor's hand, and walked away.

Later, I reminded Connor that he could always use his words, remove himself from a situation, or seek help. And that yes, if there was no other option, he could defend himself. I do not believe anyone should endure pain at the hands of another. But I also believe that most situations can be de-escalated if we know how to regulate our own emotions first.

I want to be honest though, I was mad. I judged that mother. I thought, *What is wrong with her? Why isn't she paying attention?* My protective instincts were in full force. But as we walked away, I felt terrible for those thoughts.

Later, I reflected. I remembered her saying that they had just moved to the area. She seemed tired, overwhelmed, and distracted. Her younger child was cranky. Her older child was dirty in a way that suggested more than just play. And that child? He was looking for attention. He paused before each hit, watching Connor, watching me. He was testing. Reaching. Hoping.

That moment reminded me that every behavior is communication. Every child is trying to connect. And every parent is doing the best they can with what they have and what they know. These behaviors are signals too, often misunderstood but always meaningful.

BOUNDARIES THAT EMPOWER

So what does it look like to create boundaries that empower instead of control?

- **Clarity:** Know your values and non-negotiables.
- **Consistency:** Follow through on the boundaries you set.
- **Flexibility:** Adapt when circumstances change.
- **Empathy:** Remember that children are learning, not performing.

For example, in my friend's house, they offer three food choices at mealtimes. If no choice is made, the child waits until the next meal. It is not about punishment. It is about teaching decision-making and respecting the rhythm of the household.

The hardest part is not setting the boundary, it is following through. If you set a rule but do not enforce it, you are not offering autonomy. You are offering confusion. Inconsistency sends mixed signals that children struggle to interpret.

I once had a client who struggled with this around homework. She insisted her son sit at the table until his homework was finished. He resisted, dragged it out, and the evenings became battles. Eventually, she tried something different, giving him a choice. "Do you want to do your homework before dinner or after?" To her surprise, he chose after dinner and completed it without a fight. She realized that loosening her grip and offering an authentic choice built more accountability than rigid enforcement.

PARENTING WHEN A CHILD IS BORN DIFFERENT

Boundaries take on an even deeper complexity when a child is born different. Developmental delays, disabilities, or simply ways of being that fall outside the expected mold can magnify the tension between protection and release. In those moments, the question is not only how to set boundaries, but how to trust that autonomy can flourish even when the path looks unfamiliar. This is a layer to the struggle with control that often goes unspoken.

When milestones arrive later or arrive in ways that don't match the charts in the pediatrician's office, parents often feel the urge to hold on tighter. We want to manage every detail, to shield our child from judgment, to prove to the world that they are capable. But here is the quiet tension: The more we try to control, the more we risk silencing the very autonomy that will help our child thrive.

I remember talking with a friend who said, "It feels like success is always measured against someone else's timeline." Her words stayed with me. Because the truth is, success for a child born different is not about matching the pace of others. It is about honoring their own pace. It is about redefining growth as presence, joy, and resilience, rather than comparison.

This is where boundaries become even more vital. Not boundaries that cage, but boundaries that empower. A child with delays may need more scaffolding, more patience, more repetition. But they also need the dignity of real choice, the trust that their signals matter, and the freedom to explore within safe limits. When we offer that, we teach them not only that their voice counts, but that difference is not deficiency.

And for us, the parents, it requires courage. Courage to resist the cultural narrative that says independence must look a certain way. Courage to let go of the illusion that we can control outcomes. Courage to trust that our child's path—however winding, however unconventional—is still a path of becoming.

When we parent from fear, we tighten our grip. When we

parent from trust, we loosen it with love. And in the case of children born different, that trust is not naïve. It is radical. It says: I believe in your becoming, even when the world does not understand it. I will walk beside you, not ahead of you. And I will honor your autonomy, not as a milestone to check off, but as a birthright to protect.

THE STRUGGLE WITH CONSISTENCY

I want to be truthful about something I still wrestle with. I have a hard time sticking to consistency and boundaries. I didn't have any growing up. One day it was "do this," the next it was "do what you want." That inconsistency shaped me, and even now I feel its echoes.

Part of me fears that if I stick too hard to the boundaries and house rules we have created, Connor will not give himself a break when he needs it. I see how easily he can get caught in the perfectionist's trap, and I do not want to reinforce that.

Realistically, we all have good days and bad days, calm days and turbulent ones. There are times when life feels like it's too much, and in those moments, we need to give ourselves permission to step off the gas and press the brake pedal. Sometimes we even need to pull over entirely and ask for assistance.

I know many parents who feel so overwhelmed that giving themselves a break seems impossible. Or they worry that if they stop, they will never get back on track again. I feel that too.

So the question becomes: how do we help our children navigate this decision-making process with autonomy? How do we teach them to pause with courage and self-respect, to take the break they need, but also to return with determination to the task at hand or the larger goal?

This is a balance I am still learning. Boundaries are not

meant to be rigid cages, but flexible guardrails. They should hold us steady, but also allow for the humanity of rest, recalibration, and renewal. These moments teach children to read their own internal signals of overwhelm and recovery.

NATURAL CONSEQUENTIAL DISCIPLINE

Discipline is not about punishment or rewards. It is about allowing reality to do the teaching.

Natural consequences are the outcomes that occur when a child makes a choice and experiences what follows. They are not imposed by the parent, but arise organically. If a child forgets their coat, they feel cold. If they leave their toy outside, it may get wet or lost. If they don't eat, they feel hungry. These moments build internal responsibility—not because we lecture, but because we allow the lesson to land.

But here's the hard part: Letting natural consequences unfold requires restraint. It asks us, as parents, to sit in the discomfort of watching our child struggle, knowing that the struggle is part of the growth. It asks us to resist rescuing, fixing, or softening the edges of reality. And that is not easy.

As I described earlier in the autonomy chapter, my son Connor and I had our share of "outerwear wars." At first, when he resisted wearing a coat, I would say, *"It's your body, it's your choice,"* but I still carried one along and told him, *"Just in case you change your mind."* On truly cold days, he almost always ended up taking it. On those in-between days, when it was chilly but not freezing, it was a toss-up. After a few rounds of this, I stopped bringing the coat and instead invited him to step outside and "test" the temperature for himself.

That shift, removing the safety net, was what allowed natural consequences to do the teaching. Over time, Connor became remarkably accurate at discerning his body's needs. He rarely balks at taking a coat now when he senses he will need it. Every so often he still tests the limits, but almost always he is correct. These moments weren't about autonomy alone; they were about reality itself becoming the teacher. He learned that his body would tell him when he was cold, and that ignoring those signals had real effects.

I've worked with parents who say, "But I just want to help." Of course we do. We want to protect our children from pain, frustration, and failure. But often, that impulse to help is also about soothing our own discomfort. Watching our child struggle can stir up something deep—our own fear, helplessness, and memories of being unsupported. And in that moment, it's tempting to step in, not just to ease their pain, but to quiet our own.

But our pain is not our children's to carry. It's ours to tend to. When we interrupt their struggle too quickly, we may feel temporary relief, but we also rob them of the chance to build resilience. We send the message: "I don't think you can handle this." And over time, they believe us.

Letting natural consequences unfold is not about being cold or detached. It's about being present, empathetic, and steady. It's about saying, "I'm here. I see you. I believe you can learn from this."

I once saw a story on a TV show about a little girl who kept sneaking out of bed after her parents tucked her in. The parents were frustrated and assumed she was being defiant. They responded by enforcing stricter bedtime rules. They moved lights-out earlier, added consequences, and increased supervision. But none of it worked. The natural consequence of her behavior—being tired the next day—didn't seem to change anything.

Eventually, they paused and asked a different question:

Why is she getting out of bed? That moment of curiosity led to a discovery. She was afraid of the dark. Once they added a nightlight and created a calming bedtime ritual, she stayed in bed. The boundary of bedtime remained, but it was adjusted with compassion.

This story reminds us that natural consequences are most effective when paired with reflection. If a child keeps repeating a behavior despite the consequence, it may not be defiance. It may be fear, confusion, or an unmet need. Our role is not just to let reality teach them, but to help our children understand what reality is trying to say.

Natural consequences also require discernment. Not every situation is safe to let play out. If a child runs into the street, we intervene immediately. If they are about to harm themselves or someone else, we step in. But in the everyday moments—forgetting, resisting, testing—we can often pause and ask ourselves: *Is this a moment where reality can teach my child?*

And when we do, we model something powerful: trust. We show our children that we believe in their ability to learn, adapt, and grow. That belief becomes the foundation of their self-respect.

AUTONOMY AND OWNERSHIP

So whose choice is it, really? When your child refuses to wear a coat in winter, who deals with the consequences? Ultimately, they do. And that is the point.

Our children have their own paths and choices to make. Even if they are not the choices we would make, they are still theirs. At the end of the day, autonomy is not something we hand over at a certain age. It is theirs from the start. Our role is to help them learn how to hold it wisely.

I once read a Reddit story from a mom who pushed her daughter to stay on a sports team because she did not want her to "quit." The child insisted she did not enjoy it anymore. After weeks of conflict, the mom realized she was projecting her own fear of raising a quitter. When she finally allowed her daughter to step away, she chose another activity she loved and ended up thriving. Sometimes our urge to control is rooted in our own fears of judgment, not our child's actual needs.

TECHNOLOGY AND CONTROL

Technology complicates the control and autonomy dynamic in ways no previous generation of parents has had to face. Devices can be tools, excuses, crutches, addictions, or weapons. The difference lies not in the device itself, but in how it is used, and how we, as parents, model and guide that use.

When I first became a parent, I was convinced that digital technology in the forms of TV, video games, and handheld devices would not play a major role in our household. With my background, I knew how detrimental excessive screen time could be to development. And yet, like so many families, it infiltrated our lives.

I remember the umpteenth time my son had a complete meltdown when the TV was turned off. His reaction was so intense that I realized something deeper was happening. From my studies, I understood that overstimulation can push a child into hyperarousal, the "fight, flight, or freeze" state. In that state, the frontal lobe, which governs impulse control and decision-making, goes offline. A hyper aroused child struggles to pay attention, manage emotions, follow directions, or access creativity and compassion.

And here is the thing: I began noticing these same struggles in adults. Difficulty focusing. Decision fatigue. Lack of motivation. Irritability. Impulsivity. A lack of tolerance for frustration. Could it be that our society's relationship with technology was reshaping not just our children's brains, but ours as well?

That question led me to develop a framework for evaluating technology use. I realized we could sort our digital engagement into five categories: tool, excuse, crutch, addiction, and weapon. Think of these categories as simple heuristics (mental shortcuts) to spot patterns, not formal clinical labels. They're starting points for observation, not judgments.

- **Tool:** Technology used to facilitate growth, connection, or problem-solving. A translation app that helps you connect with strangers abroad. A video call that allows grandparents to read bedtime stories across the miles. When used as a tool, technology empowers.
- **Excuse:** Technology used to justify inaction or poor behavior. "I could not finish my homework because my computer crashed." Excuses create barriers to growth and accountability.
- **Crutch:** Technology leaned on too heavily hinders or weakens long-term development. A friend of mine could not drive anywhere without GPS, even to places he had been to dozens of times. Over-reliance on a crutch limits resilience and adaptability.
- **Addiction:** Technology used compulsively, with negative consequences ignored. The endless scroll, the inability to put the phone down, the agitation when separated from a device. Addiction erodes well-being and often requires external support to reset.
- **Weapon:** Technology used to harm, belittle, or control. Cyberbullying, online shaming, or even self-weaponization,

like obsessing over "likes" and comments to determine self-worth.

As parents, our challenge is not to eliminate technology, but to help our children discern which category their use falls into. Is this device serving as a tool for connection or is it becoming a crutch that limits growth? Is this app expanding their creativity or is it functioning as an addiction that narrows their world?

And perhaps most importantly: How are **we** using technology? Children learn more from what we model than from what we say. If they see us weaponizing social media against ourselves by comparing, editing, curating, they will absorb that pattern. If they see us using technology as a tool for learning, connection, and creativity, they will absorb that too.

The truth is, technology is part of modern life, so our goal is to steward **how** it's used rather than pretend it's not there. One of the best ways to do this is to pause and ask:

- Am I using this as a tool to support growth and connection?
- Or am I using it as an excuse, a crutch, an addiction, or a weapon?

When we teach our children to ask these same questions, we give them a compass for navigating the digital world with autonomy and integrity.

A friend of mine once shared how she took away her son's tablet after repeated arguments about screen time. He exploded in anger. Later, she realized the device was his way of connecting with a friend after their family had moved to a new town. Instead of a blanket ban, they created a family rule. Devices were to be put away during meals and before bed, but could be used for social connection at certain times. The shift from punishment to connection changed everything. It shifted the signal she was sending, from "I need to control you" to "I want to understand you."

SIGNALS FOR REFLECTION: TECHNOLOGY EDITION

- When my child resists turning off a device, do I respond with control or do I pause to consider whether overstimulation is at play?
- Do I model technology as a tool for learning, connecting, and creating, or do my children mostly see me using it as a distraction?
- Have I noticed myself leaning on technology as a crutch, such as GPS dependence or constant scrolling, in ways that limit my own growth?
- Are there signs of addiction in my household, such as agitation when separated from devices, compulsive checking, or neglect of other activities or responsibilities?
- Have I or my children ever used technology as a weapon to shame, compare, or belittle ourselves or others?
- What small shifts could I make this week to reframe technology use in my home as a tool for connection rather than a source of disconnection?

RECONNECTION STRATEGIES

The goal is not just to disconnect from devices. It is to reconnect with each other.

- **Create tech-free zones or times of day:** One family I know has a basket by the door. Every evening, all devices go into the basket during dinner. At first, the kids resisted, but soon they looked forward to the uninterrupted conversations and laughter that followed.

- **Share meals without screens:** In my client's home, they have a ritual of asking one question of the day at dinner. Sometimes it is silly, sometimes it is deep, but it always sparks connection.
- **Invite conversation and play:** In our home, we started a weekly family game night. It was not about winning or losing, but about creating a rhythm of joy and presence. Now there are other nights when my son asks to play board games rather than reaching for the TV remote, because it feels like a safe, connected space.
- **Model presence and attention:** I know a father who did a personal digital detox every Sunday. He told his kids, "I'm putting my phone away because I want to be with you." The children noticed, and soon they began suggesting activities they could do together.

These strategies are not about perfection. They are about small, intentional moments of reconnection that remind our children, and ourselves, that relationships matter more than screens. These moments also send powerful signals about what we value and how we choose to show up for one another.

SIGNALS FOR REFLECTION

- Notice when you feel the strongest urge to control your child. What emotion is underneath that urge—fear, frustration, embarrassment, a desire to protect, or something else?
- Reflect on the boundaries you have set. Are they clear, consistent, and values-based, or do they shift depending on your mood or convenience?

- Consider your follow-through. Do you hold steady when a boundary is tested, or do you sometimes give in, bribe, or punish out of exhaustion?
- Think about your own relationship with autonomy. How comfortable are you with making and owning your own choices? How does that influence the way you allow your child to make theirs?
- Ask yourself: Where can I create more opportunities for my children, my family, and my community to increase genuine connection?

CLOSING THOUGHTS

Control is not about dominance. It is about creating a container where autonomy can flourish. It is about teaching our children to trust themselves by showing them that we trust them too.

When we parent from fear, we teach our children to fear themselves. When we parent from trust, we teach them to trust themselves.

As I shared earlier, I think of this as the "psychic umbilical cord"—the invisible tether that stretches but never severs. In early childhood it is close and strong, but as our children grow, it lengthens. Our role is not to cut it, but to honor it, to loosen it with love, and to trust that it will remain even as they move farther into their own becoming.

And one more thing: Give yourself grace. You will make mistakes. You will overstep, underreact, hold on too tightly, or let go too soon. You will wrestle with your own need for control, and sometimes you'll lose that battle. That doesn't mean you've failed. It means you're human.

The goal is not perfect control. The goal is conscious repair. It's modeling what it looks like to reflect, apologize, and recalibrate. When we show our children that we can own our missteps and return with intention, we teach them to do the same.

True grace is not about avoiding responsibility, it is about carrying it with kindness. It begins with how we treat ourselves, with the same compassion we hope our children will one day offer themselves.

And just as importantly, grace extends outward. It is how we honor the unique becoming of our children, whether their path unfolds along familiar milestones or takes shapes the world does not expect. Parenting a child who was born different reminds us that autonomy is not a checklist, but a birthright. It is not about conformity, but about trust.

When we parent from fear, we tighten our grip. When we parent from trust, we loosen it with love. And in that loosening, we teach our children—all children—that their difference is not deficiency, but dignity. That their voice matters. That their becoming is worthy.

In the end, every parent faces that invisible turning point—the moment when control softens into trust, and our children step forward guided not by our grip, but by the signals we've taught them to hear within themselves.

CHAPTER 15

PARENTS HAVE FEELINGS TOO

From Reactivity to Regulation

PUTTING ON YOUR OWN OXYGEN MASK

Most of this book has focused on children's emotions and needs. But parents have feelings too. And those feelings matter.

You have probably heard the saying: "Put your own oxygen mask on first." Parenting often feels like the plane is going down, alarms blaring, passengers panicking, and you are left scrambling to keep everyone safe. In those moments, if you do not know how to regulate your own emotions, it is nearly impossible to help your child regulate theirs. Our reactions become signals—cues our children read long before they understand our words.

I remember one evening at a school "trunk-or-treat" event. The gym was packed, the music was loud, and the energy was high. I felt my own body tense as the noise rose around me. That moment reminded me how quickly my nervous system can be pulled into overwhelm, and how important it is to pause, breathe, and regulate myself first. Because in that chaos, my son was watching me more closely than anyone else.

THE COMMUNITIES THAT SHAPE US

That same "trunk-or-treat" event also revealed something else: Children are not only watching their own parents. They are watching every adult in the room.

Some parents were laughing and playing with their children, others looked drained, and a few stepped into the hallway to escape the noise. Each of those responses was a signal. Children were learning not only from their own families, but from the wider community around them.

Parenting does not happen in isolation. Our children are shaped by:

- **Family communities:** Grandparents, in-laws, and extended relatives bring their own coping styles. A grandmother who soothes with bribery, an uncle who yells when frustrated, or a cousin who models patience—all of these become part of the child's learning.
- **School communities:** Teachers, coaches, and peers shape how children see authority, belonging, and conflict.
- **Neighborhood and cultural communities:** The way neighbors greet each other, the rituals of faith or culture, the tone of local sports teams or clubs—these all send signals about what is valued.
- **Digital communities:** Social media, gaming groups, and online influencers can model both adaptive and maladaptive coping.

The deeper meaning is this: Our children are constantly cross-referencing. They compare what they see at home with what they see in the world. If we tell them, "Take a breath when you are upset," but they see us snapping at a cashier or scrolling endlessly to escape stress, they notice the contradiction. If they see us practicing regulation in the middle of chaos, they notice that too.

As parents, we cannot control every influence, but we can do two things:

1. **Choose communities with intention:** Seek out environments that align with your values.
2. **Name the signals:** When your child encounters a different coping style, talk about it. "Did you notice how Auntie tried to fix things with candy? That is one way people cope. But in our family we try to talk about feelings instead."

Parenting is not only about putting on your own oxygen mask. It is also about noticing the air your child is breathing in every room they enter. Communities shape us, and by becoming aware of those influences, we can guide our children to take in what is healthy and filter out what is not.

THE EMOTIONAL STOPGAP MECHANISM

When your child is melting down in the grocery store aisle, or pushing every button you have in the car, your body reacts. Your cheeks flush, your shoulders tense, your stomach churns. You feel embarrassed, angry, helpless. And if you do not have a way to pause, those emotions spill out in ways that do not serve you or your child.

In Chapter 10, I introduced the Emotional Stopgap Mechanism as a tool for children—a way to slow the flood of feelings so they can survive the wave and learn to regulate. The same principle applies to us as parents.

Think of it like a valve on a garden hose. The water is still flowing, but the valve allows you to pause, slow, or redirect the stream. Our emotions are the water. The stopgap is the moment we give ourselves to acknowledge what is happening before it floods out in ways that are unhelpful. That pause becomes a signal, a cue that we are choosing intention over impulse.

Here is how it works:

1. **Acknowledge the flood:** Say to yourself: *I am embarrassed. I am angry. I am overwhelmed.* Naming the feeling is the first step.
2. **Allow the ninety-second wave:** Many studies suggest the intense physiological surge of an emotion peaks within roughly ninety seconds for most people, which is why pausing can help with regulation. If you can ride that wave without reacting, you give your brain time to re-engage the prefrontal cortex, the part that handles logic, impulse control, and decision making.
3. **Turn the valve:** Once you have acknowledged the feeling and allowed the surge, you can consciously "turn the valve" to slow the flow and choose your next step. This is not suppression. It is regulation.

I remember being a child in a store with my mother. If someone cut her off in line or a cashier made a mistake, she would erupt, yelling in public. I was mortified. Later, I realized that she had never been taught how to pause and regulate. Her emotions ran the show, and I absorbed that as normal. That memory, and many others like it, are why I emphasize the stopgap so strongly. Without it, we pass on patterns we never intended to. Our reactions become the signals our children inherit.

ADAPTIVE VS. MALADAPTIVE COPING

Every human being has coping mechanisms. They are the ways we try to manage stress, regulate emotions, and get through difficult moments. Some are adaptive and help us grow stronger. Others are maladaptive and may soothe us temporarily, but ultimately create harm in the long run.

ADAPTIVE COPING

Adaptive coping strategies help us regulate without creating new problems. They move stress through the body, restore balance, and model resilience for our children.

- **Physical outlets:** walking, boxing, dancing, knitting, or even tapping your foot to music.
- **Creative outlets:** painting, journaling, cooking, or playing music.
- **Relational outlets:** talking with a trusted friend, asking for help, or simply sitting with someone who listens.
- **Mind-body practices:** breathing exercises, mindfulness, prayer, meditation or stretching.

MALADAPTIVE COPING

Maladaptive coping often feels effective in the moment, but it either avoids the real issue or can create new ones if relied on repeatedly.

- **Explosive outlets:** yelling, slamming doors, or lashing out.
- **Avoidant outlets:** endless scrolling, binge-watching, or numbing with food or alcohol.
- **Rigid control:** micromanaging every detail or demanding perfection.

These strategies often show up when our stress has nowhere to go. I've been there myself. I once found myself stuck in traffic, overwhelmed and frustrated. I screamed and slammed my hand on the steering wheel. In that instant, a sharp pain shot through my chest. I thought I was having a heart attack. It turned out I had pulled a muscle in my sternum. My body was literally telling me, "This is not working."

WHY THIS DISTINCTION MATTERS FOR PARENTS

Children are watching. They are not only listening to what we say about emotions, they are absorbing what we do with our own. If they see us scream when we are angry, they learn that screaming is a way to cope. If they see us take a breath, go for a walk, or pick up a paintbrush, they learn that too.

The deeper truth is that coping is contagious. Our children borrow our strategies until they develop their own. Which means every time we choose an adaptive outlet, we are not only helping ourselves, we are also handing them a tool they can carry into adulthood. These choices become the signals that shape their own emotional habits.

THE GRAY AREA

It is also important to acknowledge that coping is not always black and white. Some strategies can be adaptive in moderation and maladaptive in excess. For example:

- Watching a show to relax can be adaptive. Using it every night to avoid feelings or connection with others can become maladaptive.
- Having a glass of wine with dinner can be neutral. Using alcohol to numb stress consistently can become harmful.
- Checking social media to connect with friends can be adaptive. Scrolling for hours to escape reality can be maladaptive.

This is why awareness matters more than perfection. The question we need to ask ourselves is not: *Am I coping the right way?* Rather it is: *Is this strategy helping me move through stress, or is it keeping me stuck?*

FOSTERING HEALTHY COPING

Once we can see the difference between adaptive and maladaptive coping, the next step is to practice building healthy skills. Awareness alone is not enough. Coping skills are like muscles—they grow stronger with use.

- **Get curious:** Explore what works for you. Maybe it is painting, knitting, tap dancing, or boxing. Play is not just for children. Adults need outlets too.
- **Practice outside the storm:** Do not wait until you are in crisis to try a new tool. Practice breathing, journaling, or stress relief exercises in calm moments so they are more established and available when you need them.

- **Use your hands:** Humans are wired to use our hands. Activities like drawing, carving, or even fidget tools can help regulate the nervous system.
- **Seek support:** Sometimes we do not know what we do not know. A therapist, coach, or trusted objective guide can help you explore healthier strategies.

REDIRECTION VS. AVOIDANCE

Coping is not just about what we do in the heat of the moment. It is also about the signals we send to our children. Two stories illustrate this contrast.

REDIRECTION IN ACTION

One afternoon, on the way to boxing practice, Connor was in the back seat, overstimulated and buzzing with energy. He began repeating the word "balls" over and over again. At first it was just noise, but then it became clear he was also playing with the inappropriate meaning of the word. Carl and I grew frustrated. We just wanted Connor to stop.

But overstimulation and impulse do not work that way. When a child is flooded, their brain is not in a place to simply switch gears because we demand it. And when the words they choose carry inappropriate undertones, it can feel even more urgent for us as parents to shut it down.

Instead of escalating, I leaned in with redirection. "If you're going to talk about balls," I said, "let's add a word to make it clear. Sports balls. Basketballs, footballs, baseballs." That small shift gave him a path forward. He began naming different kinds of balls, and the tension in the car softened.

The deeper meaning is this: Children cannot simply flip

a switch when they are overstimulated, and neither can we. Regulation is not about suppression. It is about giving energy and impulses a channel to flow through. Redirection teaches children that their words and feelings are not inherently wrong, but that they can be guided into healthier, more appropriate expressions. These moments teach them to read the internal signals of overwhelm and the external signals of guidance.

AVOIDANCE IN ACTION

A client once shared with me how, in moments of conflict, she often tried to soothe her child with quick fixes like bribery. If her child was upset, she might offer candy or a toy to distract them. It came from love—she wanted peace, she wanted to see her child happy, and she wanted the tension to dissolve quickly.

But this type of response reveals the hidden message that discomfort should be avoided rather than worked through. The child learns that the way out of hard feelings is not to feel them, but to cover them up.

Even well-intentioned adults can model maladaptive coping. And this is why our awareness matters. Because children are not only learning from us, they are learning from every adult in their orbit. When they see bribery, avoidance, or suppression in use, they absorb those strategies as acceptable. When they see patience, redirection, and calm presence, they absorb those too.

THE TAKEAWAY

Both stories reveal the same truth: Children need guidance, not suppression. Redirection gives them a channel to move through their emotions. Avoidance teaches them to bypass the discomfort altogether. Our role as parents is not to eliminate the hard feelings, but to model how to face them with compassion, creativity, and resilience.

When we practice adaptive coping in front of our children, we become living demonstrations of resilience. We show them that stress is not something to fear, but something we can move through with intention. Every signal we send, in our tone, our choices, our pauses, and our presence, becomes part of the emotional blueprint they carry forward.

SIGNALS FOR REFLECTION

- In moments of chaos, like at a school event or noisy gathering, how do I regulate myself first so my child sees me modeling calm?
- What signals are my children receiving from the communities we are part of—family, school, neighborhood, digital spaces? Which of those signals align with our values, and which need to be named and discussed?
- Do I model adaptive coping strategies or do my children mostly see me using maladaptive ones?
- Which of my coping strategies fall into the "gray area"—sometimes adaptive, sometimes not—depending on how often or why I use them?
- Take inventory: List your top three go-to coping strategies. For each one, ask yourself: *Does this help me move through stress, or does it keep me stuck?*
- When my child is overstimulated or using inappropriate words, do I tend to suppress, avoid, or redirect? How might I lean more into redirection?
- When I see other adults using quick fixes like bribery or distraction, do I talk with my child about what they noticed and how our family approaches discomfort differently?

- What outlets bring me calm and joy? How often do I practice them outside of stressful moments so they are available when I need them?
- How can I model curiosity and play in my own life so my children see that adults can explore and grow too?
- When I reach for a glass of wine, a screen, or whatever numbs the moment, am I soothing stress or reinforcing a habit that could become unhealthy?

CLOSING THOUGHTS

When we practice adaptive coping in front of our children, we become living demonstrations of resilience. We show them that stress is not something to fear, but something we can move through with intention. Every signal we send—in our own regulation, in the communities we choose, in the ways we redirect rather than avoid—becomes part of the legacy we hand to our children. Children don't need flawless parents; they need ones who are steady, attuned, and present. And presence, practiced regularly, is what teaches our children that they too can face discomfort, regulate their emotions, and grow stronger on the other side.

And while our children are always watching, the work begins within us.

Parents have feelings too. And those feelings matter. When we acknowledge them, regulate them, and model healthy coping, we give our children a gift far greater than any lecture. We show them what it looks like to be human, to feel deeply, and to recover with grace. The goal is not perfection. The goal is practice. Every time we pause, breathe, and choose an adaptive response, we strengthen our own resilience and teach our children to do the same. Grace is not the absence of accountability, it is the presence of compassion. And it begins with how we treat ourselves.

CHAPTER 16

THE RISK OF SUCCESS, ONE STEP AT A TIME

Grace in Letting Go, Strength in Small Steps

THE PARADOX OF PARENTING WELL

Parenting is often described as the most important job we'll ever have. Yet unlike most jobs, the measure of success is bittersweet. True success means our children grow into independent, capable people who no longer need us as they did in childhood. That independence is the goal, but it can also feel like heartbreak when we realize we are less central to their daily lives.

In a recent discussion with a friend, I uncovered this paradox: When we succeed, we also face loss. The risk of success is that our children will fly—and we must learn to release them with grace.

Letting go is not a single moment. It is a series of small steps, each one requiring courage, patience, and trust. The risk of success is that one day, they will not look back for reassurance. They will simply go. These moments are often quiet signals that our children are ready to step forward, even when our hearts are still learning how to release.

FIRST STEPS AND PHYSICAL INDEPENDENCE

I remember when my son took his first steps. Like so many parents, I was filled with joy and pride. But right behind that joy was a pang of realization: He was moving away from me, literally and figuratively. These moments remind us that independence begins with the body, and each step forward is also a step away.

Every milestone—first words, first bike ride, first day of school, first drive—carries that same duality. Pride and tenderness, joy and loss. And yet, those steps are necessary. They remind us that our role is not to hold our children back, but to steady them as they move forward, then let go and trust that they've learned how to steady themselves.

"TESTICLES IN MY ELBOW" AND MENTAL INDEPENDENCE

That independence shows up in their minds too. Even when we teach carefully, children will invent, imagine, experiment with language, and combine ideas in ways we never anticipated.

When Connor was about two and a half, we were in the stage of naming body parts. I wanted him to know the real words—eyes, ears, elbows, penis, testicles—because accuracy matters. It gives children ownership of their bodies and the language to describe them.

One day, we were playing a silly game. Connor pretended there was a spider crawling on his arm. "Mommy, Mommy, there's a spider on my arm!" he said, giggling. I leaned in, pretending to nibble at his arm, and I asked, "Did I get it? Did I get the spider?"

He laughed and shook his head. "No, it's over here...by the testicles in my elbow!"

I froze for a second, then burst out laughing. "Wait a minute," I said, "you don't have testicles in your elbow!" He grinned, completely confident in his imaginative declaration.

That moment reminded me that independence isn't just about walking or talking. It's about thinking. Children will create their own connections, their own logic, and their own stories. Even when we give them the "right" words, they will experiment with them, stretch them, and make them their own.

This is part of the hidden challenge of success. As children grow, they will think differently than we do. They will surprise us, sometimes confuse us, and often delight us. Our role is not to correct every imaginative leap, but to celebrate the independence of mind that shows they are becoming their own person. These leaps are signals too, small reminders that their inner world is expanding beyond ours.

EVERYDAY EMOTIONAL INDEPENDENCE

Emotional independence doesn't arrive all at once. It often shows up in small, everyday moments long before children leave home. I remember a teenager who spoke with me after a conflict with a close friend. She was upset, but instead of asking her mother to step in or fix it, she said, "I think I need to talk to her myself."

Her mother admitted that every instinct told her to intervene—to call the other parent, to smooth things over, to protect her daughter from hurt. But she paused, took a breath, and simply said, "I trust you to handle this."

The teenager did. She had the hard conversation, repaired the friendship, and came back beaming with pride. What mattered most wasn't the outcome of the conflict, but the confidence she gained in managing her own affairs and emotions.

Moments like these remind us that emotional independence begins long before the empty nest. It grows each time a child learns to carry their own feelings, to navigate stress or disappointment, and to discover that they are capable of repair without us holding the reins.

THE EMPTY NEST AND EMOTIONAL INDEPENDENCE

Years later, independence takes on a deeper form. When children leave home, parents often feel the ache of emptiness. One mother told me how lost she felt when her children moved out. She had poured her entire identity into caregiving, and when they no longer needed her daily, she wasn't even sure she knew who she was without them.

At first, the silence of her home felt heavy. But as she began to adjust, she noticed the space it created. One afternoon, while cleaning out a closet, she came across a box of old art supplies—brushes, paints, and canvases she hadn't touched in decades. She remembered how much she had loved painting before motherhood consumed her time. Tentatively, she set up a small corner in her kitchen and began again. At first, the strokes felt awkward, but soon the colors began to flow. She told me, "It was like meeting an old friend I hadn't seen in years."

Her rediscovery became more than a hobby. It was a reminder that she was more than a mother, that her identity could expand beyond caregiving. Painting gave her joy, but more importantly, it gave her back a sense of self.

And while she was reclaiming her own passions, her children were also stepping into a new kind of independence—emotional independence. They were learning to manage their own feelings, to navigate loneliness, stress, and decision-making without leaning on her every day. This stage is not only about parents rediscovering themselves, but about children discovering that they can carry their own emotional weight. They begin to trust their own resilience, to build confidence in handling life's challenges, and to know that while their parents' love is still present, their daily emotional scaffolding now comes from within. These shifts are subtle signals that their inner resilience is strengthening.

This is where the bittersweet cost of success becomes most profound. We are not only releasing our children to fully handle their own lives, we are invited to rediscover ours once again. Success in parenting opens the door to reclaiming our autonomy. It is not just about our children's independence, it's also about our own.

CLINGING TOO TIGHTLY—THE CONTRAST

Of course, many parents find the release quite difficult. I once heard about a father whose child had just gone off to college. Instead of trusting his son's independence, he called multiple times a day: "Did you remember to register for your classes?" "Did you eat?" "Did you finish your homework?" His intentions were loving, but the effect was suffocating.

This kind of constant checking is often rooted in fear: fear of not being needed, fear of losing connection, fear of mistakes. Yet clinging too tightly can backfire. It can make children feel mistrusted or—worse—incapable of managing their own lives.

As another parenting coach and I explored together, we came to understand that the risk of success is not that our children will fail without us. It is that we must learn to trust the foundation we have already laid. Independence requires space.

When we hover, we limit growth. When we release with grace, we allow confidence to expand.

LETTING GO WITH GRACE

We want our children to thrive, but we also want to remain needed. Stepping back does not mean disappearing. It means shifting roles. The balance is learning to move from managing their lives to mentoring, guiding, and finally, witnessing.

This transition can feel disorienting. For years, our identity has been intertwined with theirs. We have been the ones to soothe their tears, celebrate their victories, and carry their burdens. When they begin to carry those burdens themselves, it can feel as though we are losing our place. Yet what is really happening is a reshaping of the relationship.

Letting go with grace requires trusting the groundwork we've already set, even when we are no longer reinforcing it every day. It is the quiet confidence that the lessons we modeled—resilience, kindness, responsibility—are now woven into their own choices. Emotional independence is not about severing ties. It is about children learning to regulate their own feelings, to navigate loneliness, stress, and decision-making without leaning on us at every turn.

And while they are learning to stand in their own emotional strength, we are invited to stand in ours. We can honor their autonomy while also nurturing our own. We can rediscover passions we set aside, reclaim friendships we let drift, and remember that our identity is larger than the role of parent.

Grace is found in the small gestures. The phone call that says, "I'm here if you need me," without demanding details. The quiet pride in watching them stumble and rise again. The willingness to step back so they can step forward. It is not about absence. It is about presence in a new form—steady, spacious, and trusting.

Their growing emotional independence is mirrored by ours. As they learn to carry their own feelings, we learn to carry our own identity beyond parenting.

RECLAIMING YOUR OWN PATH

When our children step into their own lives, we are welcomed to step back into ours. Reinhabiting our own life is part of the parenting journey. This is not abandonment. This is expansion. Expansion becomes real when we pause and reflect.

So now I invite you to ask yourself:

- What passions have I postponed while in my parenting role?
- What relationships have been left untended that I may want to rejuvenate?
- What dreams have been waiting patiently, boxed away?

Success in parenting opens the door to coming home to yourself. This season of life is an opportunity to rediscover purpose and joy that are not dependent on your child's daily presence.

ONE STEP AT A TIME

Parenting is not about sweeping transformations. It is about incremental steps, practiced repeatedly. Some strategies will come easily. Others will take time, trial, and course correction.

When we try to change too much too fast, we overwhelm ourselves and our children. Sustainable growth happens in small, manageable steps. Progress over time is still progress.

Owning our mistakes is part of this process. When we are transparent with our children about our missteps, we model resilience and repair. We show them that imperfection is not failure, but part of learning.

Support from others also matters. Sometimes perspective from a friend, a partner, or a community helps us see that we are not alone in the struggle. Parenting is not meant to be a solitary journey.

SIGNALS FOR REFLECTION

- Do you feel both proud and tender when your child makes independent choices?
- Are you beginning to explore new interests, friendships, or creative outlets? Revisiting prior ones?
- Are you able to support your child at this next stage without overstepping or rescuing?
- Are you practicing patience with yourself, allowing progress to unfold gradually?
- Do you allow yourself to be transparent about mistakes and open to repair?

CLOSING THOUGHTS

Parenting is not about perfection or control. It is about guiding, releasing, and trusting. Success is not measured by how tightly we hold on, but by how gracefully we let go, one step at a time.

As you watch your child step into their own life, remember that you are invited to step into yours as well. Each small act of patience, each moment of honesty, each gentle release is part of the legacy you are building. You are not losing your child. You are witnessing their becoming. And in that becoming, you are becoming too. Their independence is not the end of your story, but the beginning of a new chapter in yours. And within that new chapter, the signals of growth continue to unfold in their own quiet way.

AN EVERLASTING LEGACY

The Investment Every Parent Needs to Make

"As a parent, what is the one thing you want to **know** before you leave this world?"

Most parents assume their role is to secure financial stability or provide for physical needs. But when we dig deeper, almost every parent answers with some variation of: "I want to know that my children will be OK without me."

That "OK" is not about money or accolades. It is about emotional stability, the assurance that our children will have the tools to live wholehearted lives, even in our absence.

Because true wealth is in the emotional investment we make in our children.

I experienced this truth with my father. In his final days, I sat by his side and told him, "Abba, I will be OK. I am happy with my life, so you don't need to worry about me." The next day, at noon on the dot, he took his last breath. My father, a Holocaust survivor, a man of precision and humor, left this world knowing I would be all right. That moment gave me peace, and it gave him release. Each layer becomes a signal that life is expanding around the grief rather than pushing it away.

This is the investment every parent must make: preparing our children not only for life with us, but for life without us.

FACING THE CONVERSATIONS WE AVOID

Very few families are willing to have deep emotional conversations around death, terminal illness, and loss. These talks often come in hushed tones during times of crisis, when decisions about care and finances overshadow emotional needs.

I once heard of a father who chose not to tell his children their mother was dying of cancer. He wanted to protect them, to preserve only happy memories. Yet in doing so, he denied them the chance to process their grief with her, to say goodbye, and to carry her presence into their healing.

Shielding children from loss does not protect them. It leaves them unprepared.

By contrast, another family I know chose honesty. The parents gathered their children and spoke gently about mom's illness. They gave them space to ask questions, to cry, and to sit with her in her final months. One evening, the youngest daughter brought her mother a drawing of the two of them holding hands under a rainbow. "This is us forever," she said. That simple act became a keepsake, a reminder that honesty had given her the chance to express love before goodbye.

Honesty, even when painful, cushions the blow. It allows grief to be shared, not hidden.

CHILDREN AND THE CAPACITY TO GRIEVE

When we are aware of the finite nature of something, our appreciation of it becomes magnified. Children, with their "living in the now" mentality, often have a greater capacity to be grateful in the moment. This ability gives them a healthier process for dealing with grief, ensuring that healing and acceptance happen alongside heartache.

Children are exceptionally flexible emotionally. While adults may fixate on feelings, digging into them and struggling to let go, children often accept their emotions at face value and move forward.

When my son lost his grandfather at the age of five, he expressed his grief with honesty: "It's so sad, and it hurts my heart. But maybe since Grandma and Gapka fought a lot, it's not so bad cause they won't fight anymore." Later, at the funeral, he whispered, "I love you, Gapka; I hope you loved me too." With tears on my face, I assured him that the love between them would never die, even though his grandfather was no longer here to express it.

Children do not need us to fix their grief. They need us to witness it. Giving them space to express emotions in a non-judgmental environment builds their capacity to identify, express, and process feelings safely.

This is true for children and adults alike. Real connection with others is a core component of healthy development. Our role is not to solve their grief, but to provide the tools they need to navigate it.

THE RUBBER BAND CYCLE OF GRIEF

Grief is not linear. It is like a rubber band wrapped around the heart. In the beginning, the band is pulled tight, narrowing against every breath, every thought, every movement. It feels impossible to live with that constriction.

Over time, life stretches the band. We eat another meal, we take another shower, we fold another load of laundry. We laugh at a story, we drive to work, we celebrate a birthday. Each ordinary act adds a layer of living that gently loosens the band's grip.

And then, something pulls it back again. For me, it was hearing the song "Don't Go Breaking My Heart." It was one of my core memories of my brother, Danny, from our childhood—him singing at the top of his lungs, dancing around in a superhero cape and nothing else, making me laugh until my sides hurt. That silly, joyful image would come rushing back, and with it the memories of his illness, his dying, and his death. The band snapped tight, and the ache was fresh again.

Danny wasn't my brother by blood, but he was my brother in every way that mattered. We were raised together from diapers, teased by my mother about being changed side by side. I have no memories of a life without him in it. When he was diagnosed with glioblastoma, I was one of the first to know. His wife, Kristina, and I grew closer, and though he lived many states away, I did what I could from afar. His children, in their late teens and early twenties, were well informed, and his wife was realistic about what was and wasn't possible.

Kristina told me that at the very end, their son was lying beside Danny, their daughter held his hand, she herself was on the other side, and his mother was trying to call his sister. Kristina gently said, "Lana, he needs you too." His mom put the phone down, came over, and whispered, "It's OK, Danny." Within minutes, he was gone. He had let go.

Too often in the dying experience, people need to be given permission to let go, especially from the ones holding on the hardest. Kristina called me on video, the only other person to see him in the aftermath, so I could say my own goodbye. Even now, I cry as I write this. The sorrow of that final goodbye leaves an indelible mark on my soul, in a way nothing else truly can.

That is the nature of grief. It does not shrink with time. It does not fade away or grow smaller. What changes is the life we build around it. Each bill we pay, each chore we complete, each breath we take, each moment that passes adds another layer of living. These layers cushion the pain, not by erasing it, but by surrounding it.

Grief remains, but our lives expand. The band is still there, but it is held within a larger, fuller life. With each cycle, we discover that we can carry both: the enduring presence of grief and the growing presence of life.

Because grief will always return, the best gift we can give our children is preparation. Not to erase loss, but to help them carry it with resilience and steadiness.

PREPARING FOR THE INEVITABLE

Luckily, it is never too late to begin. The best way to prepare children for loss is to weave emotional readiness into everyday life, so it sits alongside their physical and financial needs.

I remember teaching my son "self-help skills" when he was little. He didn't want to put on his shoes one morning and asked, "Why do I have to do it myself?" Instead of saying, "Because I said so," I explained, "Every person needs to know how to care for themselves, so they can do it even when no one else is around." His face softened, and though he still struggled, he began to see that practice was part of becoming capable. That small moment was about more than shoes. It was about confidence in his ability to stand on his own.

Another time, he asked me, "Mommy, you'll always be here

for me, right?" My heart ached, but I answered honestly: "No, I won't always be here, but I'll always be in your heart." He didn't stop being sad, but he accepted the truth more readily. These conversations don't fix the pain. They help children learn to carry it.

Children often ask big questions we cannot fully answer. Once, my son wondered if heaven was in the sky. I told him I believed heaven was all around us, in nature, in our loved ones, and deep in our hearts. He thought for a moment and said, "I think heaven is in the sky." I smiled and said, "OK, bud, that's cool." The conversation moved on, but the seed was planted: He could explore his own beliefs while feeling safe in mine.

Even with adult children, these conversations matter. When my mother was dying, she tried to protect me from the reality of her cancer, forgetting that I was her medical proxy. When she realized I fully understood what we were dealing with together, we cried and hugged through the truth. That day reminded me that while we can never be fully prepared for the pain of loss, honesty cushions it.

And preparation is not only emotional. It is practical too. I have seen families torn apart by decisions left unspoken, siblings arguing over care, wills, or funeral arrangements. The greatest gift we can give our loved ones is to relieve them of those burdens. Durable power of attorney, advanced directives, wills, and even funeral plans are not just paperwork. They are acts of love. They free our children to grieve without the weight of conflict.

When we love people, we prepare them. We give them the tools to carry on. But preparation is not only about our children. Sometimes it is about those who raised us.

PARENTING OUR PARENTS

Some might call this caregiving rather than parenting, since our parents are already adults. But for me, the experience felt like parenting: I was making decisions, holding emotional space, and guiding them through the final stage of life.

I first encountered this reversal of roles with my own parents. Before I ever became a parent to my son, I was stepping into that role with them. Both of them faced cancer, and in their final seasons of life I became caregiver, advocate, and emotional anchor.

It was humbling, it was profound, and it was sacred.

I was honored to be able to do it, yet I questioned everything—every choice, every decision, every concern. I tried to balance what I knew about each of their personalities, their wants and needs, while also carrying the weight of medical realities and end-of-life care.

That experience reshaped how I see the life cycle. It taught me that generations are deeply integrated. The child becomes the caregiver, the parent becomes the one cared for. This integration is vital for our humanity, but it also complicates the work of breaking generational traumas. We are asked to honor the past even as we try to do things differently for the future.

Parenting our parents is not the same as parenting our children. Our children are still learning who they are; our parents have already lived, gathered wisdom, and formed identities. Some adults never fully know themselves, but it is not our role to tell them who they are. It is our role to take them at their word, to honor their wishes, even when they differ from what we would choose for ourselves.

That distinction changes how we show up: with respect, reverence, acceptance, and fortitude. It is their life to live out as they wish. And in caring for them, I learned that legacy is not only what we pass forward, but also how we honor those who came before us.

MOVING FORWARD WITH LOSS: REMEMBERING AS LEGACY

Caring for my parents reminded me that legacy is lived in both directions. We prepare our children for life without us, and—in the normal course of things—we prepare ourselves for life without our parents. That duality—carrying grief while carrying forward their stories—is what moves us into the work of remembrance.

Legacy is lived not only in plans such as securing our children's future through documents and directives, but in memory as well. In gestures, humor, voices, and rituals. It's in the stories we tell, the traditions we keep, and the ways we remember. These fragments live alongside the sorrow, both held together in the same heart.

My father's accent was like a leftover stew: Polish, German, Hebrew all mixed together. He spoke with his hands as much as with his voice—every story punctuated by sweeping gestures, every opinion carried on the rhythm of his movements. One evening at the dinner table, I playfully held his hands down against the table. To my surprise, he couldn't get his words out. Without his hands, his voice faltered, as though his gestures were the language itself. That moment makes me laugh even now, but it also reminds me how deeply his presence shaped me, how even his quirks became part of the way I remember him.

My mother, facing cancer, met complication after complication. Doctors repeatedly said, "This is so unexpected." Her reply: "Well, nobody ever expected the Spanish Inquisition."

Humor became her coping mechanism, her way of staying herself even as illness took her away.

And sometimes remembrance comes in unexpected ways. A few months after my father's death, I stumbled upon an old voicemail from him. Hearing him say my name was an all-consuming moment of anguish and joy. I was wracked with sobs, collapsing onto my bed. Carl rushed in, thinking something terrible had happened. In truth, something had: Grief had returned with full force, reminding me of the depth of my loss. Yet even in that heartbreak, there was gratitude. His voice was still here, captured in a fragment of technology, a reminder that legacy lives not only in stories but in sounds, gestures, and the traces of everyday life.

These moments live on in me. They are my inheritance. And they remind me that legacy is not only cultural, like *Zachor*, the Jewish act of remembrance, it is personal. We relive those we have lost in the stories we tell, the humor we recall, the voices we hear again, and the lessons we carry forward.

THE RIPPLE EFFECT OF EMOTIONAL INVESTMENT

Whether we are parenting our children or parenting our parents, the emotional investments we make ripple outward. They shape not only the immediate family but the wider community, leaving traces of resilience and compassion that extend far beyond our own lifetime.

When we model resilience in our homes, it flows outward. A child who learns to face grief honestly may one day comfort a friend through loss. A colleague who sees us navigate hardship with humor may find courage to do the same. Even small acts—a kind word, a moment of honesty, a gesture of love—multiply, becoming part of a collective inheritance.

The lessons we share, even the ones learned through hardship, become part of a wider pattern. This is how we create an everlasting legacy.

SIGNALS FOR REFLECTION

- How do I talk with my child about loss—do I shield them, or invite them into honesty?
- What signals do I send about grief: Do I model avoidance, or do I show that feelings can be held and carried?
- In what ways am I preparing my child not only for life with me, but for life without me?
- How do I honor the legacy of those who came before me, and what fragments of memory do I want my child to carry forward?
- What practical steps (documents, directives, rituals) can I take now to ease the burden of loss for my family later?

CLOSING THOUGHTS

As we reflect on loss and legacy, it is important to remember that these themes are not separate from the everyday signals we send our children. The way we model honesty, presence, and resilience in the face of death becomes part of the emotional scaffolding they carry throughout their lifespan. Just as signals shape their earliest experiences of autonomy and empathy, they also shape how they grieve, how they remember, and how they continue the story long after we are gone.

Loss is inevitable, but legacy is intentional. Grief will come, but so will resilience. Pain will resurface, but so will laughter. Legacy is not only what we leave when we die. It is how we live now, with presence, humor, and love.

Every story we tell, every act of integrity, every moment of love becomes part of the inheritance our children will carry. And in the end, that is the most enduring legacy of all.

Sometimes it's the smallest fragments that stay with us: a silly song, a familiar voice, a shared joke, a hand held in silence. These fragments live alongside the sorrow, both held together in the same core of who we are. This is the paradox of grief; it does not shrink, but our lives grow around it, making space for both the ache and the joy.

The deepest peace a parent can carry is knowing their child can stand without them. And the deepest honor a child can carry is knowing they stood beside their parents when it mattered most. Grief is the shadow of love, and legacy is its light. Together, they remind us that while loss is inevitable, the way we live now is the inheritance we leave behind. And the signals we send in the way we live become the quiet threads our children will follow long after we are gone.

ACKNOWLEDGEMENTS

This book would never have been possible without the consistent, reassuring support of my incredible, dynamic business manager, Jessamyn Overly; the early stage enthusiasm and approval of Jared Rosen from DreamSculpt Books & Media; the empathetic guidance and encouraging assistance of my book coach, Mattie Murrey-Tegels; the incredibly diligent skills of my editor, Lori Doyle; the loving generosity and meticulous final copyedits and proofreading of my sister, Mori Sokal; the truly generous friendship, unerring support and resources of David Goldberg, owner of Edge Studio where my audiobook was recorded; and the meticulous and vehement backing of my publisher, Scribe Media. I also want to extend a special thank you to Don Huff, the graphic designer of my book cover for capturing my wild and unorthodox imagination and putting it into print. Lastly, but certainly not least, to my family, friends, clients, colleagues, mentors and communities for supporting my journey, through the messiness and madness that is the book writing process.

RECOMMENDED READING & RESOURCES

CURATED BOOKS, AUTHORS, AND ORGANIZATIONS TO SUPPORT YOUR PARENTING JOURNEY

These books and resources were selected because they align with the themes of *Unspoken Signals*: emotional safety, connection, autonomy, resilience, developmental insight, and the everyday practice of raising emotionally secure children. Each recommendation is parent-friendly, research-grounded, and deeply supportive of the work you're doing in your home.

PARENTING, EMOTIONAL DEVELOPMENT & CONNECTION
THE WHOLE-BRAIN CHILD

Daniel J. Siegel & Tina Payne Bryson A clear, neuroscience-based guide to understanding children's emotional and behavioral responses. Offers practical tools for connection and co-regulation.

NO-DRAMA DISCIPLINE

Daniel J. Siegel & Tina Payne Bryson A compassionate approach to discipline that focuses on teaching, not punishing, and helps parents understand the brain behind behavior.

PARENTING FROM THE INSIDE OUT

Daniel J. Siegel & Mary Hartzell An exploration of how your own childhood experiences shape your parenting—a powerful companion to the reflective work in your book.

THE POWER OF SHOWING UP

Daniel J. Siegel & Tina Payne Bryson A parent-friendly explanation of attachment and the four S's: safe, seen, soothed, and secure.

RAISING GOOD HUMANS

Dr. Carla Naumburg A practical, compassionate guide to breaking reactive cycles and building mindful, connected relationships with children.

THE EVOLUTION OF PARENTING (PODCAST)

Yarona Boster and Robert Hulse A conversational podcast exploring how parenting evolves across generations, blending insight, experience, and real-life stories. https://evolutionofparenting.podbean.com/

RESILIENCE, AUTONOMY & COMPETENCY
THE SELF-DRIVEN CHILD

William Stixrud & Ned Johnson A powerful exploration of autonomy, motivation, and the science behind giving children appropriate control over their lives.

THE GIFT OF FAILURE

Jessica Lahey A compelling case for allowing children to struggle, learn, and grow—essential reading for parents navigating independence.

HOW TO RAISE AN ADULT

Julie Lythcott-Haims A research-backed look at overparenting and how to foster independence, resilience, and confidence.

LET GROW (ORGANIZATION)

A nonprofit dedicated to promoting independence and resilience in children. Offers free resources, school programs, and parent tools. www.letgrow.org

EMOTIONAL INTELLIGENCE & COMMUNICATION
THE EMOTIONAL LIFE OF THE TODDLER

Dr. Alicia F. Lieberman A beautifully written, developmentally grounded look at early childhood emotions and the parent-child bond.

THE GOTTMAN INSTITUTE (EMOTION COACHING RESOURCES)

Research-based tools for helping children understand and manage emotions through validation and connection.

PERMISSION TO FEEL

Marc Brackett, PhD A guide to building emotional intelligence in families, schools, and communities, grounded in the Yale Center for Emotional Intelligence's research.

THE LANGUAGE OF LISTENING: 3 SIMPLE STEPS TO TRANSFORM FAMILY LIFE

Sandra R. Blackard A simple, powerful communication framework that aligns beautifully with your signals-based approach.

TRAUMA, HEALING & INTERGENERATIONAL PATTERNS
THE BODY KEEPS THE SCORE

Bessel van der Kolk, MD A foundational text on trauma, the nervous system, and healing. Dense but transformative for understanding emotional patterns.

WHAT HAPPENED TO YOU?

Bruce D. Perry, MD, PhD & Oprah Winfrey A compassionate, accessible exploration of trauma, resilience, and the power of connection.

IT DIDN'T START WITH YOU

Mark Wolynn A parent-friendly introduction to intergenerational trauma and how patterns are passed down—and changed.

CHILD DEVELOPMENT & BEHAVIOR
HOW CHILDREN DEVELOP

Robert S. Siegler et al. A comprehensive but accessible overview of developmental psychology across childhood.

THE SCIENCE OF PARENTING

Margot Sunderland A neuroscience-informed guide to understanding children's emotions and behaviors.

CENTER ON THE DEVELOPING CHILD (HARVARD UNIVERSITY)

A leading source for research on early childhood development, executive function, and resilience.

TEMPERAMENT, INDIVIDUAL DIFFERENCES & PERSONALITY
RAISING YOUR SPIRITED CHILD

Mary Sheedy Kurcinka A supportive guide for parents of children with strong temperaments—sensitive, intense, persistent, or highly active.

THE HIGHLY SENSITIVE CHILD

Elaine N. Aron, PhD A foundational resource for understanding sensory sensitivity and emotional intensity in children.

SOCIAL-EMOTIONAL LEARNING (SEL)
CASEL (COLLABORATIVE FOR ACADEMIC, SOCIAL, AND EMOTIONAL LEARNING)

The leading organization defining SEL competencies and offering research-backed tools for families and schools.

THE WHOLE-BRAIN CHILD WORKBOOK

Siegel & Bryson A practical companion to SEL development through stories, exercises, and reflection.

PARENTING WITH MINDFULNESS, PRESENCE & COMPASSION
EVERYDAY BLESSINGS: THE INNER WORK OF MINDFUL PARENTING

Myla & Jon Kabat-Zinn A reflective, grounding guide to parenting with presence and compassion.

SIMPLICITY PARENTING

Kim John Payne & Lisa M. Ross A gentle, thoughtful approach to reducing overwhelm and creating emotional spaciousness for children.

FOR PARENTS WANTING DEEPER THEORY

SELF-DETERMINATION THEORY: BASIC PSYCHOLOGICAL NEEDS IN MOTIVATION, DEVELOPMENT, AND WELLNESS

Deci & Ryan A foundational academic text behind the connection–autonomy–competency framework.

ATTACHMENT IN PSYCHOTHERAPY

David J. Wallin A deeper dive into attachment theory and its lifelong impact.

THE DEVELOPING MIND

Daniel J. Siegel A comprehensive exploration of interpersonal neurobiology and how relationships shape the brain.

RESOURCES INDEX

A Parent-Friendly Guide to the Psychological, Developmental, and Communication Frameworks Referenced in This Book

A

ATTACHMENT THEORY

Developed by John Bowlby and Mary Ainsworth, this theory explains how children form emotional bonds with caregivers. Consistent, responsive care leads to secure attachment, which supports confidence, emotional regulation, and healthy relationships.

AUTHORITATIVE PARENTING

A parenting style identified by Diana Baumrind that blends warmth with firm boundaries. Research consistently shows it produces the most resilient, emotionally secure children.

AUTONOMY (SELF-DETERMINATION THEORY)

One of the three core psychological needs identified by Deci & Ryan. Autonomy refers to a child's need to feel a sense of choice, agency, and ownership over their actions.

B

BAUMRIND'S PARENTING STYLES

A foundational framework describing four parenting styles: authoritarian, authoritative, permissive, and uninvolved. These styles reflect different combinations of warmth and structure.

BANDURA'S SOCIAL LEARNING THEORY

Albert Bandura's research showing that children learn by observing others. Tone, body language, reactions, and emotional patterns are absorbed long before children can explain what they see.

BOWEN FAMILY SYSTEMS THEORY

A framework describing how family members influence one another's behavior. Patterns often repeat across generations unless intentionally changed.

C

CASEL SEL COMPETENCIES

The Collaborative for Academic, Social, and Emotional Learning identifies five core skills: self-awareness, self-management, social awareness, relationship skills, and responsible decision-making.

CENTER ON THE DEVELOPING CHILD (HARVARD UNIVERSITY)

A leading research center focused on early childhood development, executive function, and the science of resilience.

CO-REGULATION

The process by which a calm, regulated adult helps a child return to emotional balance. This is the foundation of emotional safety and emotional learning.

COMPETENCY (SELF-DETERMINATION THEORY)

A core psychological need referring to a child's sense of capability and effectiveness. Children thrive when they feel "I can do this."

CONNECTION (SELF-DETERMINATION THEORY)

The need to feel loved, valued, and emotionally safe with caregivers. Connection is the foundation of secure attachment and resilience.

CULTURAL PARENTING NORMS

The understanding that parenting styles and expectations vary across cultures and communities, shaping how children interpret authority, autonomy, and emotional expression.

D

DEVELOPMENTAL CASCADES

A concept describing how early experiences influence later development. Small patterns—positive or negative—can accumulate over time.

DEVELOPMENTAL DOMAINS (EARLY CHILDHOOD)

Widely used in early childhood education: physical, cognitive, language, social-emotional, and adaptive/self-help development.

E

EARLY CHILDHOOD DEVELOPMENT

The study of how children grow across physical, cognitive, emotional, and social domains from birth through age eight.

EMOTION COACHING (GOTTMAN)

A parenting approach that teaches children to understand and manage their emotions through validation, naming feelings, and guiding problem-solving.

EMOTIONAL CONTAGION

The phenomenon where emotions spread between people. Children often "catch" a parent's stress, calm, or frustration within seconds.

EMOTIONAL REGULATION THEORY

Research describing how children learn to manage big feelings. Regulation develops through co-regulation, modeling, and practice—not punishment.

EXECUTIVE FUNCTION SKILLS

Cognitive skills including working memory, impulse control, and flexible thinking. These develop slowly and require supportive environments.

F

FAMILY STRESS MODEL

A framework showing how parental stress affects children's emotional and behavioral outcomes. Stability and support buffer these effects.

G

GOODNESS OF FIT (TEMPERAMENT THEORY)

The match between a child's temperament and their environment. Children thrive when parenting aligns with their natural traits.

GROWTH MINDSET (DWECK)

The belief that abilities can grow with effort and practice. Children with a growth mindset show greater resilience and persistence.

I

INTERGENERATIONAL TRAUMA

The transmission of trauma across generations through behavior, emotional patterns, and sometimes biology. Awareness helps break cycles.

INTERNAL WORKING MODELS

Mental templates children form about themselves and others based on early caregiving experiences. These shape future relationships.

INTERPERSONAL NEUROBIOLOGY (SIEGEL)

A field exploring how relationships shape the brain. Secure, attuned relationships support healthy neural development.

L

LET GROW

A nonprofit organization promoting independence, resilience, and age-appropriate autonomy in children. Letgrow.org

M

MENTALIZATION/REFLECTIVE FUNCTIONING

The ability to understand behavior—your own and your child's—as communication driven by internal thoughts and feelings.

N

NEUROPLASTICITY

The brain's ability to change and grow throughout life. Supportive environments can reshape patterns and strengthen resilience.

P

PARENTING STYLES (MACCOBY & MARTIN)

An expanded version of Baumrind's model that further clarifies the dimensions of warmth and control.

PERMISSIVE PARENTING

A style characterized by warmth without boundaries. Children may feel loved but lack structure and predictability.

PLATINUM RULE (ALESSANDRA)

"Treat others the way *they* want to be treated." In parenting, this means attuning to your child's unique needs and temperament.

POLYVAGAL THEORY (PORGES)

A theory explaining how the nervous system responds to safety and threat. Children's behavior often reflects physiological states, not intentions.

R

RESILIENCE THEORY ("ORDINARY MAGIC")

Dr. Ann Masten's research showing that resilience grows through everyday protective factors like stable relationships and emotional safety.

S

SCAFFOLDING (VYGOTSKY)

Supporting children just enough to help them grow without taking over. This aligns with the Zone of Proximal Development.

SELF-EFFICACY (BANDURA)

A child's belief in their ability to succeed. Self-efficacy grows through mastery experiences and supportive feedback.

SELF-DETERMINATION THEORY (DECI & RYAN)

A framework identifying three core needs—connection, autonomy, and competency—that support motivation, resilience, and emotional security.

SOCIAL AND EMOTIONAL INTELLIGENCE

Skills that help children understand emotions, manage reactions, read social cues, and build healthy relationships.

SOCIAL LEARNING THEORY

Bandura's theory that children learn by observing others. This is central to the concept of "signals."

T

TEMPERAMENT THEORY

Research showing that children are born with biologically based temperament traits. Parenting becomes more effective when aligned with these traits.

W

WINDOW OF TOLERANCE (SIEGEL)

The range in which a child can stay regulated. Outside this window, they move into fight, flight, or freeze and need co-regulation.

Z

ZONE OF PROXIMAL DEVELOPMENT (VYGOTSKY)

The "learning sweet spot" where a child can succeed with just the right amount of support. Too much help or too little both hinder growth.